INTEGRATING AI IN THE CLASSROOM

INNOVATIVE METHODS TO OPTIMIZE LESSON PLANNING, SAVE TIME GRADING, AND ENHANCE STUDENT ENGAGEMENT

J.H. MADRON

CONTENTS

INTRODUCTION

Struggling to balance teaching and non-teaching duties is a daily juggle for many educators. Take Sarah, a dedicated English teacher who spends countless hours grading papers, planning lessons, and attending meetings. Yet, shockingly, teachers like her spend just under half their week directly engaging with students. Imagine that!

According to recent data, a whopping 78% of educators feel crushed under the weight of administrative tasks, dampening their spirits (Henebery, 2023). It's disheartening to hear that teachers, whose passion lies in nurturing young minds, are buried in paperwork and accountability demands. Your dedication deserves more support and recognition.

THE LEAP INTO AI AND INTEGRATION HESITATIONS

As educators, you're juggling a multitude of responsibilities every single day. From planning engaging lessons to attending meetings, grading assignments, and handling administrative duties, it's easy to feel overwhelmed. Your time is valuable, and effectively managing all these tasks can pose a real challenge.

One of the most significant pain points you face is the time-consuming nature of grading and assessment. It's no secret that pouring over piles of assignments can eat into your valuable time, leaving you with less room to focus on the more complex aspects of teaching and learning. But what if there was a solution? Imagine having AI tools that could automate routine grading tasks, freeing up your time and energy for more meaningful interactions with your students.

Another challenge you encounter is meeting the diverse learning needs of your students. With varying learning styles, paces, and abilities in a single classroom, providing personalized support can feel like an uphill battle. But fear not because, with the right strategies and tools, you can create an inclusive learning environment where every student feels valued and supported on their educational journey.

Data overload is yet another hurdle you must navigate as an educator. You must collect data on student performance to track progress and pinpoint areas for improvement effectively. However, the sheer volume of data can quickly become overwhelming without practical tools for analysis. You can utilize technology to access essential insights from your data, enabling you to make informed decisions and improve your teaching strategies.

As if these challenges weren't enough, the educational landscape constantly evolves, with new technologies and teaching methods emerging. Staying current and adjusting your methods to suit the needs of modern learners is essential. Integrating AI into your teaching toolkit can help you stay ahead of the curve and embrace the opportunities that come with change.

While the responsibilities and challenges you face as an educator may seem daunting, know you're not alone. By leveraging the power of AI and staying adaptable in the face of change, you can overcome these obstacles and continue to inspire and empower your students every step of the way.

HOW TECHNOLOGY, ESPECIALLY AI, CAN TRANSFORM TEACHING

Imagine this: With the power of AI, you could reclaim up to 30% of your time currently consumed by administrative tasks (*How AI*, 2023). That's precious time you could invest back into what truly matters—your students—no more drowning in paperwork or grading marathons. Instead, you can focus on nurturing meaningful connections with your students, understanding their unique needs, and tailoring your teaching approach to help them thrive.

This book is about more than just reducing your workload. It's about embracing technology, particularly AI, to open up new teaching horizons. Thanks to universal access, consider offering innovative teaching approaches that cater to all learning styles and abilities. The options are limitless, from personalized learning journeys to interactive simulations and instant feedback systems.

Indeed, it's essential to recognize that not all applications of AI in education hold the same value. While it has the potential to revolutionize teaching, we must also be mindful of how we implement it. As one expert aptly puts it, AI isn't just about automating existing teaching methods—it's about creating entirely new ones. So, let's embrace this opportunity to reimagine education and usher in a new era of teaching that's truly transformative.

What drew you to this book? Perhaps you're feeling overwhelmed by the demands of teaching in today's digital age, longing for a way to reclaim your time and reignite your passion for education. Or you're curious about the possibilities that technology holds for the future of teaching. No matter the cause, understand that you have companionship on this journey. Together, let's navigate the exciting terrain of technology in education and empower ourselves to shape the future of teaching for the better.

BENEFITS OF READING THIS BOOK

Discover the ultimate guide to seamlessly incorporating AI into teaching and administrative tasks, saving time and effort. This book offers a comprehensive roadmap, ensuring hassle-free integration of AI to streamline your responsibilities.

Reading this will unlock shortcuts to automating tasks, enhancing efficiency, and enriching the learning experience. Dive into practical strategies for leveraging AI tools, minimizing administrative burdens, and maximizing instructional impact. Bid farewell to laborious manual tasks and welcome a streamlined approach to education. Embrace the future of teaching with confidence, knowing you have a trusted resource at your fingertips.

WHO IS THIS BOOK FOR?

This book is specifically for educators like you who are enthusiastic about seamlessly integrating AI into their classroom dynamics to enhance the learning experience. Whether you're a seasoned educator or just starting, if you're seeking a guide that can empower you to harness the potential of AI to support both yourself and your students, this is for you. Discover practical strategies and insights tailored to your needs to enhance teaching effectiveness and student engagement. Embrace this resource as your ally in creating an innovative and dynamic educational environment.

HOW TO USE THIS BOOK

When diving into this book on AI integration in education, kick things off with the first chapter. It lays down the fundamental groundwork for AI's role in education, setting you up for a solid understanding of how AI can enhance your teaching experience.

Once you've got that foundation, you're in for a treat with the six AI-integration methods waiting for you. What's fantastic is that you can address them in whatever order best fits your requirements!

First up, you've got "Method 1: Streamlining Lesson Planning." This chapter is about making your lesson planning smoother than ever with the power of AI. Say goodbye to the countless hours of brainstorming and embrace innovative strategies to take your teaching skills to the next level.

Next, "Method 2: Enhancing Exam and Activities Creation." Here, you'll discover how AI can breathe new life into your exam and activity creation process. It's all about crafting assessments that measure understanding and spark engagement and creativity in your students.

Then, "Method 3: Revolutionizing Grading and Assessment." Get ready to wave goodbye to stacks of papers to grade! With AI, grading becomes quicker, more personalized, and more effective, giving your students the feedback they need to excel.

In "Method 4: Researching New Teaching Materials and Methods," you will embrace the future of education by tapping into AI's ability to unearth the latest teaching resources and methods tailored just for you and your students.

"Method 5: Providing One-to-One Support for Students" is next on the list. With AI by your side, you can personalize the learning journey for each student, meeting them where they are and helping them reach their full potential.

Last but not least, "Method 6: Automating Administrative Tasks." Bid farewell to tedious administrative duties as AI steps in to streamline your workflow, giving you more time to focus on what truly matters: teaching.

So, whether you're eager to streamline your lesson planning, revolutionize your grading process, or explore new teaching methods, there's something for everyone in this book. Explore and unlock the game-changing potential of AI in education right now!

WHAT YOU'LL GAIN FROM THIS BOOK

Reading this book will transform your teaching journey, providing newfound efficiency and effectiveness. By implementing the methods within, you'll discover a surplus of time to dedicate to your true passion: teaching. Imagine seamlessly integrating AI tools into your classroom, amplifying your ability to connect with students and facilitate more profound learning experiences.

Before this innovative approach, navigating teaching demands was arduous, with little time spared for personal growth or innovative methods. Now, with this resource, you'll feel confident and equipped to navigate the educational landscape easily. This is the perfect book to empower and elevate your teaching practice.

CHAPTER 1

EDUCATION IN THE AGE OF AI

I magine entering your classroom, where AI tailors each lesson to your student's unique learning styles. One day, a struggling student's eyes light up—AI identified his challenge and adapted the material just for him. Suddenly, he's not just keeping up; he's excelling. This is the strength AI brings to education.

THE ROLE OF TECHNOLOGY IN SHAPING EDUCATION FORWARD

Technology has reshaped the educational landscape in ways we could hardly have imagined a generation ago, ushering in a new era where traditional methods meet digital innovation. As an educator, you stand at the forefront of this transformation, navigating through an ever-evolving array of tools and strategies to enhance learning. Let's dive into how technology is shaping and actively propelling education forward.

Gone are the days when your role was solely the "sage on the stage," where you were the primary fountain of knowledge, and students passively absorbed information. Today, technology invites you to adopt the role of a "guide on the side." This shift empowers students to take charge of their learning journey, using digital resources to explore, discover, and learn at their own pace and style. It's a vibrant, interactive approach where you facilitate, support, and inspire rather than instruct.

Imagine a classroom where every student engages with the lesson in a way that suits their learning preferences. Visual learners can watch an animation, auditory learners can listen to a podcast, and kinesthetic learners can participate in interactive simulations. This is not a futuristic vision—it's today's reality, enabled by technology.

Educational platforms and apps have made learning more accessible than ever before. Students in remote areas or those who need flexibility due to personal circumstances can now access quality education online. Meanwhile, educational games and virtual reality experiences turn learning into an engaging adventure, making subjects that were once dull exciting to explore.

But technology's impact doesn't stop at accessibility and engagement. It has also revolutionized the way we assess and support student learning. Adaptive learning technologies customize educational content for each student's needs, providing personalized routes to mastery. Real-time feedback mechanisms allow you to spot and address learning gaps swiftly, ensuring that every student can succeed.

Moreover, technology has prepared students for a digital future, equipping them with the critical 21st-century skills they need to thrive. From digital literacy to problem-solving in virtual environments, students are learning to navigate the complexities of a connected world. As educators, you're teaching subject matter and mentoring digital citizens.

As technology advances, it promises to take on an increasingly significant role in education. Emerging trends like AI and machine learning offer glimpses of a future where educational experiences are even more tailored, immersive, and effective. The potential for technology to further personalize learning, automate administrative tasks, and even predict educational outcomes could revolutionize how we approach teaching and learning.

However, adopting these changes involves more than just embracing new tools; it demands a shift in mindset. As educators, you're encouraged to be lifelong learners, constantly exploring new technologies and pedagogical strategies to enhance your teaching. Networking with fellow educators, attending professional development workshops, and staying updated on the latest educational technology trends are all crucial steps in this journey.

Technology's impact on education is undeniable. It has shifted the roles of teachers and learners, made education more accessible and engaging, and prepared students for the future. As educators, you play a pivotal role in harnessing the power of technology to create meaningful and compelling learning experiences. Remember, in the digital age, your mission is to educate, inspire, guide, and empower the next generation of learners. Welcome the transformation, delve into the opportunities, and join hands to forge the future of education.

A Technology Timeline Showing How Innovation and Technological Advancements Have Transformed Education Over the Years

As an educator, you're on the front lines of witnessing how technology reshapes the learning landscape. Let's journey through a "Technology Timeline" to appreciate the milestones that have revolutionized education, making your role more impactful yet challenging in navigating these changes.

- **The dawn of digital education (1980s–1990s):** Imagine a classroom in the late 20th century where the chalkboard reigned supreme. Then, suddenly, computers began to creep into the corners of these rooms. The Apple II, introduced in the late '70s, became a beacon of educational technology, bringing interactive learning experiences into the classroom. This era laid the groundwork for digital literacy, transforming how you teach basic subjects, from math with fun software like Math Blaster to typing skills with Mavis Beacon Teaches Typing.
- **The rise of the internet (1990s–2000s):** As the internet went from a government tool to a household necessity, classrooms worldwide felt its impact. The late '90s and early 2000s saw the rise of educational websites and resources, making information more accessible than ever. You no longer had to rely solely on textbooks for information, as a wealth of knowledge became available at the click of a mouse. This period democratized education, allowing for a more

personalized learning experience and introducing the concept of distance education.

- **Interactive whiteboards and smart classrooms (2000s):** Gone were the days of chalk dust and squeaky markers with the advent of interactive whiteboards in the early 2000s. These tools made lessons more engaging and catered to various learning styles. Visual learners could benefit from dynamic presentations, while kinesthetic learners could interact with the content physically. You could save and share lessons digitally as an educator, enhancing the collaborative learning experience.

- **The tablet and smartphone era (2010s):** The introduction of tablets and smartphones brought about a new level of personalization in education. Apps and e-books allowed for learning not just confined to the classroom but could happen anywhere and anytime. Tools like Kahoot! made assessments fun and engaging, while resources like Khan Academy provided free tutorials on various subjects, supporting differentiated instruction and self-paced learning.

- **The age of AI and machine learning (2020s):** Today, you stand at the cusp of an educational revolution powered by AI and machine learning. Personalized learning has gone beyond apps and games; AI algorithms can now analyze a student's learning habits, strengths, and weaknesses to tailor content accordingly, potentially offering a custom education plan for each student. Machine learning can predict learning outcomes and provide insights into improving teaching strategies.

- **Looking ahead:** As we look to the future, virtual and augmented reality promise to make immersive learning experiences commonplace, breaking down the classroom walls to explore ancient civilizations, dive into the human bloodstream, or visit distant planets without leaving the desk.

For educators, this timeline isn't just a testament to technological progress; it's a map of the evolving landscape of education. To embrace these changes, you must be open-minded and willing to learn. As daunting as it may seem, remember, at the heart of all these advancements is the goal to enhance learning and teaching. By leveraging these technologies, you're not just keeping up with the times but empowering your students to reach their full potential in this ever-changing world.

DEMYSTIFYING AI IN EDUCATION: UNDERSTANDING THE BASICS

AI transcends being merely a trendy term; it's a potent influence transforming multiple industries, notably education. Essentially, AI encompasses machines or software that emulate human intelligence, executing tasks and refining their capabilities through the data they acquire. For educators like you, this means a new era of teaching and learning that's more personalized, efficient, and dynamic.

Let's journey through AI's timeline and see how its milestones have directly influenced education. From the 1950s, when AI was a fledgling concept, to the 1980s and 1990s, when machine learning and neural networks began to take shape, each advancement brought us closer to today's intelligent, adaptive learning environments. In the 2000s, AI became mainstream as data mining and natural language processing improved educational software. Now, in the 2020s, AI is integral to creating personalized learning experiences, automating administrative tasks, and offering insights into student performance that were previously unimaginable.

So, why AI, out of all the technological advancements? Its unique strength comes from the rapid and precise analysis of vast data volumes. This capability is crucial in education, where understanding each student's learning style, preferences, and challenges can significantly impact their academic journey. AI can tailor learning experiences to individual needs, making education more accessible and effective for everyone.

AI's role in modernizing education is multifaceted. It's not just about more innovative algorithms or data processing; it's about revolutionizing how we approach teaching and learning. AI streamlines the grading process, freeing up your time to concentrate on teaching rather than paperwork. It also offers students immediate feedback, making their learning experience more interactive and captivating. Furthermore, AI-driven analytics can predict student performance, allowing for early interventions to help students stay on track.

The potential of AI to equalize opportunities in education stands out as one of its most thrilling aspects. With AI-powered tools, students from various backgrounds can access personalized tutoring, language support, and resources that might not be available in their immediate environment. This democratization of education helps bridge the gap between different socioeconomic groups.

Moreover, AI is leading the forefront in transforming education because it continuously evolves. As AI technology improves, so does its application in education, promising an ever-enhancing learning experience. Imagine a future where AI tutors provide students with personalized learning paths, making education a truly tailored experience. We're not far from this reality, with AI already being used to develop virtual mentors and tutors that adapt to individual learning speeds and styles.

AI profoundly transforms education, presenting an unparalleled chance to revolutionize teaching methods and learning experiences. It makes education more tailored, accessible, and streamlined. As educators, embracing AI means keeping up with technology and leading the charge in creating a future where every student has the tools they need to succeed. Welcome to the exciting era of AI in education—teaching and learning have never been more thrilling!

AI Technology and Their Application in Education and Teaching

Dive into AI technology and discover how it's revolutionizing education and teaching. As an educator, you possess robust tools to improve your teaching techniques and more actively engage your students. Let's explore some groundbreaking AI technologies and their real-life applications in education.

- **Machine learning (ML):** Machine learning algorithms customize the learning journey for each student based on their unique needs. Platforms like Coursera utilize machine learning to assess students' performance and tailor the curriculum, ensuring personalized attention to areas requiring enhancement. Picture a classroom where every student embarks on a tailored educational path that leverages their strengths and addresses their weaknesses.

- **Generative AI:** This technology is making waves by creating new content, from automated essay feedback to generating quiz questions. Tools like GPT (Generative Pre-trained Transformer) can give students instant feedback on their written assignments, allowing you to focus on in-depth, personalized coaching. It's like you have an assistant for grading, freeing your time for more creative teaching.

- **Learning management systems (LMS):** LMS platforms like Canvas and Blackboard integrate AI to offer more intuitive and responsive learning environments. They can automatically suggest resources to students based on their course interactions and performance, making learning resources more accessible and tailored. This approach ensures students stay engaged and supported throughout their educational journey.

- **Simulations with VR/AR:** Virtual and augmented reality (VR/AR) are taking simulations to the next level. These technologies create immersive learning experiences that were once unimaginable. For example, medical students can gain valuable hands-on experience by practicing surgeries in a risk-free virtual environment, avoiding real-world consequences. This is a game-changer for practical learning in fields where experience is everything.

- **Natural language processing (NLP):** NLP technology transforms students' interactions with educational content. Chatbots and virtual assistants can comprehend and reply to students' questions in natural language, assisting around the clock. This means students can get assistance whenever needed, breaking down barriers to learning outside the classroom.

These AI technologies are not just futuristic concepts but fundamental tools you can use to elevate your teaching and make learning more engaging and personalized for your students. While this overview scratches the surface, it opens a window into the possibilities AI brings to education. Embrace these technologies, and you'll find innovative ways to inspire and educate your students like never before.

A LOOK INTO PROMPT ENGINEERING BASICS FOR YOU

Building on the foundational knowledge you've gained in the previous section, let's step into the next dimension of utilizing AI in education: prompt engineering. This idea revolutionizes our interaction with AI, making learning more captivating and efficient.

So, what exactly are prompts? Think of them as conversation starters or questions you pose to AI, designed to elicit specific information or responses. Based on your educational objectives, these prompts can vary from straightforward questions to intricate directions.

You can use prompts for a wide array of purposes. They're tools for sparking creativity in writing assignments, solving math problems, generating quiz questions, or creating interactive learning scenarios. The sky's the limit when you know how to craft the correct prompts.

Where do these prompts come into play? Primarily in AI-powered platforms like ChatGPT and its alternatives, such as OpenAI's GPT-3, Google's Bard, or Anthropic's Claude. Each platform has unique strengths but thrives on well-designed prompts to deliver valuable and relevant responses.

Understanding how to make well-designed prompts is crucial. A good prompt directs the AI to produce responses that are not only accurate but also tailored to your students' learning levels and interests. For example, a well-crafted prompt for a creative writing assignment might be, "Write a short story about a space adventure, including a twist ending, for a 10th-grade reading level." This prompt provides clear guidance on the task's scope and expected complexity.

Conversely, a lousy prompt, such as "Write a story," lacks specificity and direction. Without context or criteria, the AI's response may be too vague or advanced, missing an educational opportunity.

The difference between good and bad prompts becomes more evident with practice. Good prompts lead to engaging, educational content that sparks curiosity and learning, while bad prompts result in generic, unhelpful responses.

By embracing prompt engineering, you position yourself at the cutting edge of educational innovation. Mastering this skill allows you to customize AI interactions to fit your curriculum, making learning more interactive and personalized. Jump into the world of prompt engineering with excitement. It's your turn to shape the future of education, guiding your students with creativity and precision in this AI-assisted learning journey.

What Is Prompt Engineering?

Prompt engineering is an innovative approach where you, as an educator, craft questions or statements designed to elicit specific responses or behaviors from students. Consider it the skill of posing the correct questions most effectively to optimize learning results. This strategy is essential in teaching and learning, engaging students, and encouraging deep thinking and understanding.

Following best practices for crafting well-designed prompts is crucial to excel in Prompt Engineering. Here's a personalized version of the FACTS cycle to guide you:

- **Framing:** Start by framing your prompts within the context of the lesson. Ensure they are relevant, thought-provoking, and aligned with your learning objectives. For example, instead of posing the question, "What is photosynthesis?" consider asking, "How does photosynthesis demonstrate the interconnected roles of sunlight, water, and carbon dioxide?" This encourages students to think critically about the process and its implications.

- **Asking:** Your questions should be clear and concise yet open-ended to encourage exploration. Avoid yes/no questions. For example, "What role do you think renewable energy should play in our future energy policies?" This invites discussion and allows students to express their thoughts and opinions, fostering a more engaging learning environment.

- **Contextualizing:** Make your prompts relatable by linking them to real-world examples or current events. This approach helps students understand how their learning applies to real-life situations. For example, relate a history lesson to current events by asking, "How do historical conflicts inform our understanding of today's international relations?"

- **Tailoring:** Adapt your prompts to fit your student's diverse needs and levels. Consider their backgrounds, interests, and learning styles. For a lesson on narrative writing, you might say, "Write a story inspired by your favorite song," allowing students to draw on personal interests.

- **Stimulating:** Finally, ensure your prompts stimulate further inquiry and self-directed learning. Encourage students to ask their questions and pursue answers beyond the classroom. For instance, after a lesson on ecosystems, ask, "What local environmental issue interests you, and how can you learn more about it?"

Incorporating these practices into your teaching creates a more interactive, student-centered learning environment.

This makes learning more enjoyable and effective as students engage deeply with the material.

YOUR ROLE IN THE AI ERA

In the heart of the AI-education dialogue stand you, the teacher, a pivotal figure navigating an evolving landscape of pedagogical strategies and technological advancements. Your grasp of fundamental AI concepts and prompt engineering doesn't just add to your skill set; it empowers you, aligning seamlessly with your ever-evolving responsibilities. It's about enhancing your role, not overshadowing it, transforming how you teach and students learn.

Let's consider how AI is reshaping your role. Instead of viewing AI as a competitor for attention or a replacement, imagine it as a highly efficient teaching assistant (TA). This TA doesn't call in sick, tirelessly churns out personalized learning material, and provides real-time feedback to students, allowing you to focus on what you do best—teaching, mentoring, and inspiring.

The collaboration between you and AI systems should be synergistic, not antagonistic. AI can handle data analysis, grading, and even identifying student learning patterns, which can be incredibly time-consuming. This partnership allows you to dedicate more time to developing creative lesson plans, engaging in one-on-one interactions, and fostering a supportive classroom environment that encourages critical thinking and problem-solving.

Consider AI as a teaching assistant, a resource that enhances the learning experience while preserving the crucial human aspect of education. It's about leveraging AI to create more interactive, personalized learning experiences. For instance, AI can help tailor lesson plans to meet the unique needs of each student, identifying areas where they struggle and adapting the curriculum accordingly. A few decades ago, this degree of personalization seemed impossible, but now, AI puts it right at your fingertips.

Furthermore, embracing AI in education means acknowledging its role in preparing students for a future where digital literacy is non-negotiable. By integrating AI into your teaching practices, you're not just enhancing education; you're equipping your students with the skills they need to thrive in an increasingly digital world.

Embark on this new journey with the understanding that AI in education aims not to replace you but to augment your capabilities and enrich the learning experience for both you and your students. It's an exciting time to be an educator, with endless possibilities to explore how AI can improve teaching and learning. So, as you stand at the forefront of this revolution, embrace AI as your ally in crafting the next generation of learners, thinkers, and leaders.

KEY TAKEAWAYS

- You are central to integrating AI into education, enhancing their role rather than being replaced by leveraging AI for personalized student learning experiences.
- AI redefines your role by acting as a teaching assistant, handling tasks like data analysis and

grading, thus allowing you to focus on creative and interactive teaching methods.

- Collaboration between you and AI should be synergistic, with AI providing support in developing tailored lesson plans and identifying student learning patterns for a more personalized education.
- AI systems are tools for enhancing learning experiences, not your replacements, emphasizing the importance of human interaction and your irreplaceable value in the educational journey.
- Integrating AI in teaching practices prepares students for a digital future, equipping them with essential digital literacy skills needed in an increasingly technological world.
- The use of AI in education opens up possibilities for personalized learning, real-time feedback, and a more efficient and engaging educational process, highlighting the transformative potential of AI in reshaping how education is delivered and experienced.

We've just seen how AI can transform your teaching, making it more effective and engaging. Let's take it further with "AI-Integration Method 1: Streamlining Lesson Planning." Discover how AI enhances learning outcomes and simplifies your preparation process, giving you more time to inspire.

CHAPTER 2

AI-INTEGRATION METHOD 1— STREAMLINING LESSON PLANNING

You're up late again, scrolling through endless resources, trying to piece together a lesson plan that sticks. It's that familiar tug-of-war between meeting curriculum standards and engaging every student. Coffee in one hand, determination in the other, you're committed to making learning come alive despite the daunting task ahead. But there's a silver lining. With AI, you can tailor lesson plans that hit the mark every time, making your job much easier.

WHERE AI FITS IN LESSON PLANNING

You're likely familiar with the numerous challenges of lesson planning. It's a time-consuming task that often involves hours of preparation to develop lesson designs that effectively teach designated skills. Imagine streamlining this process to make it more efficient and engaging for you and your students. This is the potential of integrating AI into lesson planning.

Why Integrate AI Into Lesson Planning?

Integrating AI into lesson planning brings a wide range of advantages:

- **Time-saving:** AI tools can significantly reduce the time spent on administrative tasks and lesson creation, allowing you to focus more on engaging with your students and enhancing their learning experiences.
- **Accessibility:** AI tools ensure that all students, no matter their physical or cognitive abilities, have access to learning opportunities, making education more inclusive.
- **Improves student engagement:** By tailoring learning experiences to individual interests and preferences, AI-powered tools can boost student engagement and motivation.
- **Easy content generation:** AI can effortlessly generate quizzes, tests, homework assignments, and other educational materials that are customized to meet the learning objectives and curriculum goals.
- **Continuous improvement:** AI models such as ChatGPT can learn from your requirements and enhance their responses, becoming more adept at providing customized and practical assistance with lesson planning.

Where and How AI Can Help

AI's capabilities and features that can assist in lesson planning include:

Streamlining instructional design preparation: By leveraging AI, you can use innovative apps like ChatGPT and Education Copilot to simplify the process of instructional design preparation, making it faster and more efficient.

Automating administrative tasks: AI can automate tasks such as creating schedules, managing student data, and even grading assignments, freeing up more time for you to focus on teaching and student interaction.

Personalizing learning content: AI tools can tailor lessons to each student's learning style, adjust the difficulty level and pace to match the student's ability, and provide real-time data to help you address learning gaps.

Using AI to Create a Lesson Plan

To leverage AI in your lesson planning, identify the specific skills or standards your lesson aims to address. Use AI tools to generate "I can" statements that articulate these learning goals in student-friendly language. You can then ask the AI for formative assessment ideas to gauge student understanding, lesson activities that align with your goals, and differentiated instruction methods to support all learners, including English language learners.

Incorporate AI tools to automate the generation of educational content and assessments, ensuring they align with your learning objectives. Utilize AI's ability to analyze student data for personalized learning recommendations and to identify areas where early intervention is needed.

Remember, as you integrate AI into your teaching methods, these technologies aim to augment your role rather than replace it. They offer innovative ways to save time, personalize learning, and improve student engagement. So, why not explore AI-powered lesson planning tools and see how they can transform your teaching and students' learning experiences?

A LOOK INTO AI-POWERED LESSON PLANS

When comparing traditional, non-AI lesson plans to those enhanced with AI, it's crucial to focus on aspects such as exhaustiveness of content, student engagement, time efficiency, and adaptability to student progress. Let's examine the critical differences between the two, using real-life examples and discussions on how AI can support you in lesson planning.

In a non-AI lesson plan, you typically focus on a structured, step-by-step approach to teaching a subject, relying heavily on traditional methods such as lectures, textbook assignments, and paper-based tests. These plans are straightforward but might not always engage all students or adapt to their learning needs.

On the other hand, an AI-powered lesson plan uses technology to enhance learning, making the process more interactive, personalized, and adaptable. For example, by incorporating AI tools like chatbots, students can engage in a 5E instructional model (Engage, Explore, Explain, Elaborate,

Evaluate) with activities tailored to their interests and learning pace. AI can help create lesson plans that are informative, engaging, differentiated, and aligned with best practices.

Moreover, technology can enhance lesson plans by integrating tools or platforms for collaborative projects, making learning more dynamic and interactive. This approach allows for a more hands-on experience where learners can use their knowledge in real-world situations, further enriching their learning experience.

Key Differences Highlighted

- **Exhaustiveness of content:** AI can sift through large data sets, ensuring your content comprehensively covers all necessary topics and skills. This contrasts with traditional plans, where your knowledge and resources limit the content scope.
- **Student engagement:** AI-enhanced lesson plans can dynamically adapt to include interactive elements, simulations, and personalized learning paths, leading to higher levels of student engagement compared to the more static and generalized approach of non-AI plans.
- **Time efficiency:** AI tools streamline lesson planning, allowing you to quickly generate and customize lesson plans, activities, and assessments. This efficiency enables you to dedicate more time to address the needs of individual students and to other teaching responsibilities.

- **Adaptability to student progress:** AI systems can adjust the difficulty level of tasks and suggest new topics based on real-time assessments of student progress, something traditional lesson plans cannot do. This flexibility guarantees that every student faces the right level of challenge and receives the support they need throughout their educational journey.

How You Can Use AI to Create a Lesson Plan

Utilizing AI to make a lesson plan involves:

- specifying your learning goals distinctly.
- crafting detailed prompts for the AI, specifying the target audience, context, and specific details of the lesson you wish to develop.
- integrating feedback mechanisms to alter the lesson plan based on learner engagement and understanding.

AI can significantly enhance lesson planning, offering a personalized, efficient, and adaptive approach to education. Integrating AI into lesson planning, despite the value of traditional approaches, can enrich students' learning experiences and make them more engaging. By leveraging AI, you can not only save time but also create lesson plans that are more aligned with the needs and abilities of your students, ultimately contributing to better learning outcomes.

AI-ENHANCED LESSON PLANNING TOOLS

Crafting engaging and effective lesson plans is essential for teaching success but often requires a lot of time and effort. Fortunately, AI tools have emerged as powerful allies, offering innovative ways to streamline each step of the lesson-planning process. Let's dive into how you can leverage these tools to design comprehensive, engaging lesson plans, focusing on the following steps:

- outlining learning objectives
- planning learning activities
- gathering learning materials
- writing out details
- organizing your work
- assessing student progress

Outline Learning Objectives With ChatGPT

Overview and Features:

ChatGPT, created by OpenAI, is a conversational AI that can comprehend and produce text resembling human conversation. It can assist in formulating clear, concise, and measurable learning objectives based on the curriculum and students' needs.

Access and Pricing:

Accessible via OpenAI's website, ChatGPT offers various subscription models, including a free tier with basic functionalities and paid options for more advanced features.

How to Use It:

- Start by providing ChatGPT with the topic and educational level of your lesson.
- Request examples of learning objectives for similar lessons.
- Use the AI's suggestions to craft objectives tailored to your students' needs.

Prompt Tips:

- Be specific about your subject and grade level to get more tailored suggestions.
- Request objectives that use Bloom's Taxonomy for measurable and achievable goals.

Pros and Cons:

- **Pros:** Instant access to various suggestions; ability to refine objectives based on feedback.
- **Cons:** It may require multiple iterations to get perfectly tailored objectives.

Plan Learning Activities With Jasper

Overview and Features:

Jasper AI specializes in content creation, making it an excellent tool for generating ideas for engaging learning activities that align with your objectives.

Access and Pricing:

Jasper can be accessed through its website, offering different subscription plans based on usage needs, including a free trial.

How to Use It:

- Input your learning objectives into Jasper.
- Request activity ideas that meet these objectives.
- Customize the suggested activities to fit your classroom dynamics.

Prompt Tips:

- Ask for activities that promote active learning, collaboration, or critical thinking.
- Request variations for different learning styles.

Pros and Cons:

- **Pros:** Generates creative and diverse activity ideas quickly.
- **Cons:** Activities may require adaptation for specific contexts or student needs.

Gather Learning Materials with Lex.page

Overview and Features:

Lex.page is a newer AI tool that helps create and share web pages. It helps compile and organize learning materials from various sources into a cohesive, accessible format.

Access and Pricing:

Accessible online, Lex.page offers free and premium subscription options, depending on the level of customization and storage required.

How to Use It:

- Use Lex.page to curate articles, videos, and other resources aligned with your lesson's objectives.
- Create a dedicated page for your lesson, organizing materials into sections or topics.

Prompt Tips:

- Include keywords or topics to find the most relevant materials.
- Ask for resources that are age-appropriate and engaging.

Pros and Cons:

- **Pros:** Simplifies collecting and organizing materials; easy sharing with students.
- **Cons:** It may require time to curate high-quality resources.

Write Out Details With Helloscribe

Overview and Features:

Helloscribe is an AI writing assistant that excels in creating detailed lesson plans, including step-by-step instructions and teacher scripts.

Access and Pricing:

Helloscribe offers various pricing tiers online, including a basic free version and premium options for more extensive features.

How to Use It:

- Input the structure of your lesson plan into Helloscribe.
- Provide details about your objectives and activities.
- Let the AI generate a comprehensive lesson script.

Prompt Tips:

- Offer precise details about each part of your lesson to get a more structured output.
- Request specific sections like introduction, main activity, and conclusion.

Pros and Cons:

- **Pros:** Saves time on writing; helps ensure all lesson components are covered.
- **Cons:** Outputs may require personalization to match your teaching style.

Organize Your Work With Bit.AI

Overview and Features:

Bit.AI is a document collaboration platform perfect for organizing lesson plans, materials, and resources in one easily accessible location.

Access and Pricing:

Bit.AI has a web interface with various plans, including a free tier for primary use and premium options for more advanced collaboration features.

How to Use It:

- Create a workspace for your lesson plans.
- Upload and organize documents, links, and other resources.
- Share access with co-teachers or students as needed.

Prompt Tips:

- Organize resources by unit or subject for easy retrieval.
- Leverage the collaboration features to gather feedback from your peers.

Pros and Cons:

- **Pros:** Centralizes lesson planning materials; facilitates collaboration.
- **Cons:** It might be more than needed for individual educators without a team.

Assess Student Progress With Knewton's Alta

Overview and Features:

Knewton's Alta is an adaptive learning platform that tailors personalized learning experiences and assessments to meet each student's needs, enabling real-time progress tracking.

Access and Pricing:

Available through its website, Knewton offers institution-based pricing so that costs will vary based on the agreement with the educational institution.

How to Use It:

- Implement Alta as part of your lesson to deliver personalized content and assessments.
- Monitor student progress through the platform's analytics.

Prompt Tips:

- Create assessments that match your learning objectives closely.
- Use data from Alta to adjust your teaching strategies.

Pros and Cons:

- **Pros:** Offers personalized learning paths and insightful data on student progress.
- **Cons:** Requires institutional buy-in; may have a learning curve for setup.

With these AI tools, you can streamline lesson planning from start to finish. For example, you can use ChatGPT to draft your learning objectives, Jasper to brainstorm engaging activities, and Lex.page to curate relevant materials. Helloscribe can help you articulate the lesson details, while Bit.AI keeps everything organized. Finally, assess your students' understanding and progress with Knewton's Alta. This seamless integration of AI into your planning process saves time and enhances the quality and effectiveness of your lesson plans.

Remember, while AI can significantly assist in lesson planning, the educator's insight, creativity, and empathy remain irreplaceable. The ultimate goal is to use these tools to complement your skills, allowing you to dedicate more time to what truly matters—inspiring and nurturing your students.

IMPLEMENTATION GUIDE FOR METHOD 1

The journey of integrating AI into your teaching practices can be as exciting as it is daunting. This guide offers actionable advice and steps to simplify the process, specifically focusing on using AI to plan lessons. Whether you're teaching kindergarten or college, the thoughtful integration of AI can enhance learning experiences, making them more interactive, personalized, and engaging. Let's explore how you can navigate this integration smoothly.

Review Your Curriculum

Begin by thoroughly reviewing your current curriculum. Identify the core objectives, the skills you aim to develop, and the knowledge you want your students to acquire. This review is crucial because it sets the stage for where and how AI can benefit most. Ask yourself: Which areas could benefit from more personalized attention? How can AI assist students in overcoming their learning challenges?

For instance, if you notice that students often struggle with complex mathematical problems, AI tools can offer personalized problem sets based on each student's learning pace. Similarly, AI can suggest reading materials for each student at the right difficulty level in language arts.

Assess Where AI Should and Shouldn't Be Implemented

Not all parts of your curriculum will benefit from AI, and that's okay. It's essential to distinguish between areas where AI can genuinely enhance learning and where traditional methods may still be the best approach. For example, while AI can provide personalized quizzes and interactive simulations, the socio-emotional aspects of learning, such as empathy and teamwork, are best developed through human interaction.

Consider the logistics and ethics of AI implementation: privacy concerns, data security, and ensuring that the technology is an aid, not a crutch. The objective is to use AI to enhance and supplement your teaching rather than substitute for the irreplaceable human element.

Start Small

Once you've identified potential areas for AI integration, start small. Choose one lesson or a single component of your curriculum to experiment with. This approach allows you to manage the learning curve and the logistical aspects of integrating new technology.

For example, you could begin by using an AI tool that helps create interactive history timelines, making the past more vivid and engaging for your students. Introduce an AI-driven grammar checker to assist students in instantly enhancing their writing skills.

Evaluate, Iterate, and Build

After implementing an AI tool, actively monitor its impact by gathering student feedback on their experiences. Assess whether they feel more engaged and better understand the material, using this feedback to evaluate the effectiveness of the AI integration.

Don't be afraid to iterate. If something isn't working, tweak it. If an AI tool isn't delivering the expected benefits, consider trying a different approach or tool. This process of evaluation and iteration is critical to successfully integrating AI into your curriculum.

Using AI to Create a Lesson Plan

Now, let's talk about how you can specifically use AI to plan lessons. Planning lessons with AI can save you time, provide new insights, and offer creative approaches to teaching and learning. Here are some modes AI can help in lesson planning:

- **Content generation:** Use AI to generate ideas for class activities, discussion topics, or project prompts. This is particularly beneficial when seeking new perspectives or strategies for tackling a topic from various viewpoints.
- **Personalization:** AI can analyze data from your students' past performances to suggest personalized learning paths. For example, it can identify which concepts need reinforcement and suggest tailored activities for each student.
- **Resource aggregation:** AI tools search the internet for educational resources to match them with your lesson objectives. This can dramatically reduce your time searching for relevant videos, articles, and interactive tools.
- **Assessment creation:** AI can help you create customized assessments that cater to your students' diverse learning needs, ensuring that quizzes and tests are fair and comprehensive.

Incorporating AI into lesson planning doesn't mean losing your personal touch or creativity. Instead, think of AI as a powerful assistant that can handle the tedious aspects of lesson planning, freeing you up to focus on the creative and interactive parts of teaching you love.

Practical Example

Imagine you're planning a lesson on climate change. An AI tool can help you gather the latest research, news articles, and scientific data. It can suggest interactive models to simulate the effects of global warming or recommend virtual field trips to places affected by climate change. With AI's help, you can create a lesson plan that's informative but also immersive and interactive, making a complex subject more accessible and engaging for your students.

Integrating AI into your teaching practices, especially lesson planning, is a journey of exploration and learning. By reviewing your curriculum, assessing where AI fits best, starting small, and being open to iteration, you can harness the power of AI to enhance your teaching and provide your students with a richer learning experience. Remember that the aim isn't to substitute you but to enhance and uphold your invaluable daily efforts. Embrace AI's possibilities, and let it inspire you to create lessons that ignite your students' passion for learning.

Keep exploring the latest research and statistics on AI in education as you progress to stay informed about new tools and best practices. The future of teaching and learning is bright with AI as your ally.

KEY TAKEAWAYS

- Integrating AI into lesson planning saves time, boosts student engagement, and delivers personalized learning experiences.

- AI tools like ChatGPT can assist in formulating clear learning objectives and generating content such as quizzes and educational materials.
- Personalization through AI allows lessons to adapt to individual student needs, improving accessibility and closing learning gaps.
- You can focus on teaching and student interaction as AI-powered tools automate administrative tasks.
- AI enhances lesson plans by providing exhaustive content, increasing student engagement, improving time efficiency, and offering adaptability.
- AI should be implemented by reviewing the curriculum, assessing where AI fits, starting small, and iterating based on feedback.
- AI is positioned as a tool to augment your work, not to replace it, aiming to complement your creativity and empathy in the learning process.

Having explored how AI can transform your lesson planning, let's dive into method 2 in the next chapter. Like the tools that streamline your planning, AI can similarly revolutionize how you craft exams and activities, seamlessly blending the personal touch you bring to teaching with the efficiency and customization AI offers.

CHAPTER 3

AI-INTEGRATION METHOD 2—ENHANCING EXAM AND ACTIVITIES CREATION

Creating exams and activities puts you in a tough spot, trying to balance challenging your students while keeping everything fair. AI emerges as your ally, offering personalized assessments and instant feedback. Embrace its transformative power to tailor tasks, foster engagement, and nurture individual growth. Let AI be your guide in empowering learners.

RETHINKING YOUR QUIZZING PRACTICES

You often rely on quizzing as a vital tool in your teaching arsenal to assess students' understanding, reinforce learning, and provide feedback. Usually, quizzes stick to conventional formats like essay questions, short answers, true/false, and multiple choice. Although these approaches have proven effective, their drawbacks can limit students' ability to learn and stay engaged. Recognizing these limitations and exploring how AI can revolutionize quizzing practices can lead to more inclusive, interactive, and practical learning experiences.

Traditional Quizzing Practices and Their Limitations

Traditional quizzes often emphasize memorization over comprehension, encouraging students to recall information rather than understand and apply concepts. This can lead to superficial learning, where students focus on short-term memorization instead of long-term retention and skill development. Additionally, these quizzes may not accommodate different learning styles, posing challenges for some students in effectively showcasing their knowledge. They can also be time-consuming to create and grade, especially for essay questions, limiting the immediate feedback crucial for learning.

Moreover, traditional quizzes often don't provide personalized feedback or adapt to individual learning paces and needs. A universal approach might discourage students who require extra time to understand specific concepts or who would thrive by engaging with more complex questions. The lack of personalization and adaptability can result in missed opportunities for deeper learning and engagement.

The Importance of Rethinking Quizzing Practices

In the era of AI, the educational landscape is rapidly evolving. AI has the potential to transform quizzing practices from static assessments into dynamic, interactive learning activities. This transformation is not just beneficial; it must prepare students for a future where critical thinking, creativity, and adaptability are paramount. Rethinking quizzing practices with AI integration can enhance learning outcomes by making quizzes more engaging, personalized, and inclusive.

AI-powered quizzes can adapt to a student's performance in real time, offering easier or more challenging questions based on their answers. This approach to adaptive learning makes sure every student, no matter their skill level, faces the right amount of challenge and support, leading to a more profound grasp of the subject matter.

Moreover, AI can deliver immediate, customized feedback, identifying strengths and determining enhancement areas. This immediate response helps students reflect on their learning process, encouraging a growth mindset and fostering a more engaging and interactive learning experience.

Transforming Quizzing Practices With AI

Imagine quizzes where every question adapts to each student's learning pace, style, and needs. AI makes this possible by analyzing student responses in real time, offering personalized paths through the material. This flexibility supports various learning styles and fosters fairness, enabling every student to thrive, no matter their background or preferred ways of learning.

AI can also transform quizzes into interactive activities. Picture a scenario where students engage with a virtual lab simulation as part of a quiz, applying theoretical knowledge to practical experiments. This hands-on approach deepens understanding and retains interest, moving beyond traditional assessments to immersive learning experiences.

Furthermore, AI-driven analytics can uncover trends and pinpoint areas where students face challenges, offering insights into individual and class-wide performance. This data can inform teaching strategies, allowing for targeted interventions and support where needed most.

The Road Ahead

Keeping the human aspect central is essential when incorporating AI into your quiz-making practices. AI tools should complement, not replace, the invaluable human interaction and guidance you provide. Balancing technology with a personal touch ensures that quizzing remains a meaningful and supportive part of the learning journey.

Integrating AI into quizzing practices also requires a willingness to experiment and learn. Not every AI tool will fit every classroom or subject matter; trial and error are necessary to find what works best for you and your students. Stay informed about the latest developments in educational technology, and don't hesitate to seek out resources and training to enhance your understanding and implementation of AI in your teaching practices.

Rethinking your quizzing practices with AI is more than just a shift in methodology; it's a step toward a more inclusive, engaging, and effective educational future. Adopting AI enhances your students' academic journeys and equips them for a future where technology and adaptability are intertwined. Let's embark on this journey together, reimagining what quizzing can be and unlocking the full potential of every student.

AI-ENHANCED EXAM AND ACTIVITIES CONTENT GENERATION

AI tools have become invaluable assets in the dynamic world of education, where the goal is to teach and engage. For you, the educators looking to revolutionize the way you design exams and create interactive activities, there's a plethora of AI-powered tools at your disposal. Let's dive into how these tools can transform your teaching methods, focusing on generating diverse exam questions and crafting engaging student-centric activities.

Generating Diverse and Customized Exam Questions

Objective Tests

▶ **Multiple-choice and true-false:**

- **Quizgecko and Quizbot:** These platforms excel in creating multiple-choice and true-false questions. By leveraging AI, they can generate questions based on your content, ensuring a broad range of topics and difficulty levels. Access these tools online, with Quizgecko offering free primary usage and Quizbot available through subscription plans. Input your content. The AI will suggest further questions you can customize. Their user-friendly interfaces make question generation a breeze but ensure the review of the AI-generated questions for accuracy and relevance.

▶ **Matching and problem-based questions:**

- **PrepAI:** Specializes in creating more complex question types like matching and problem-based questions. Available online, PrepAI offers various pricing tiers, including a free trial. You feed the AI with your syllabus or specific topics, and it crafts questions tailored to your needs. Its strength lies in generating problem-solving questions ideal for subjects requiring critical thinking. While it offers customization options, it's essential to fine-tune the difficulty level to match your students' capabilities.

Subjective Tests

▶ **Essay and short answer:**

- **OpExams and Questgen:** These tools are champions in crafting essay and short answer questions. OpExams provides a flexible pricing model online, including a complimentary version with basic features. Questgen, similarly available online, provides a subscription-based model. Both tools require you to input critical topics or learning objectives, and they generate comprehensive essay prompts or short answer questions. These platforms are great for developing critical thinking and expression skills among students. However, it's crucial to personalize the prompts to align with your course objectives and the student's current learning stage.

Creating Engaging, Interactive, and Student-Centric Activities

Homework, Assignments, Group, and Individual Activities

- **EdApp and Testportal:** EdApp shines in creating interactive assignments and homework. It's a mobile-first learning management system (LMS) that integrates gamification into learning. You can access EdApp online, with pricing varying based on your desired features and scale. Testportal, in contrast, emphasizes using interactive tests and quizzes tailored for group and individual activities. Through a subscription model, it provides various question types and instant feedback.
- **Fillout's Quiz Maker and Toolsaday:** For more customized activities, Fillout's Quiz Maker allows you to create personalized quizzes that can adapt based on student responses, perfect for homework or assignments. Toolsaday offers a variety of educational tools, including interactive games and activities suitable for both group and individual learning. Both platforms function online and offer various pricing plans to meet different needs.

How to Utilize These Tools Effectively:

- **Identify your objectives:** Before diving in, clarify your aim with each tool. Is it to assess knowledge, encourage critical thinking, or enhance engagement?
- **Explore and experiment:** Spend time exploring the features each tool offers. Most platforms provide

tutorials or step-by-step guides to help you get started.

- **Customize:** While AI can generate content, the magic happens when you tailor this content to your student's needs and interests. Add unique touches to make the learning experience more suitable and pleasing.
- **Review and revise:** AI isn't perfect. Review the generated content for accuracy, relevance, and inclusivity. Adjust difficulty levels as needed to match your students' abilities.
- **Integrate feedback:** Adjust your use of these tools based on student feedback. Remember, what succeeds in one class might not be in another, so stay flexible and ready to adapt.

Pros and Cons

Pros:

- **Efficiency:** These tools can save you a tremendous amount of time in question and activity generation.
- **Diversity:** AI can help introduce a broader range of topics and question types, enhancing the learning experience.
- **Engagement:** Interactive and personalized activities can significantly boost student engagement and motivation.

Cons:

- **Accuracy:** AI-generated content may require accuracy adjustments or better match learning objectives.
- **Personalization:** While AI offers customization, it can't fully replace your nuanced understanding of their students' needs and capabilities.
- **Cost:** Some tools may be expensive, especially for full-featured access, which can be a barrier for some educators.

Incorporating these AI tools into your teaching practice can transform how you assess and engage your students. Using their capabilities, we can create a learning environment that is more dynamic, inclusive, and effective. Remember, the goal is not to replace you but to augment and enhance the teaching process, making education more accessible, personalized, and impactful for every student.

IMPLEMENTATION GUIDE FOR METHOD 2

Integrating AI interventions into your teaching practices can revolutionize how you engage with students, personalize learning, and manage classroom tasks. This guide will walk you through practical steps to seamlessly incorporate AI tools into your existing curriculum, ensuring you leverage the benefits while maintaining the integrity of your educational goals.

Review Your Curriculum

Start by taking a thorough look at your curriculum. Understand the core objectives, the skills you aim to develop in your students, and the knowledge they need to acquire. This step is vital as it helps us identify the most effective strategies for utilizing AI. For instance, if critical thinking and problem-solving are essential components of your course, AI-driven simulations and problem-solving environments can offer students hands-on experience in a controlled yet dynamic setting.

Assess Where AI Should and Shouldn't Be Implemented

Not every aspect of your curriculum will benefit from AI, and that's okay. It is essential to identify where AI can enhance learning outcomes and where its application might detract from the learning experience. For example, AI can provide personalized learning paths, instant assignment feedback, and automated grading for multiple-choice tests. However, the human touch remains irreplaceable in discussions that require emotional intelligence, empathy, or moral judgment. Remember, AI should augment your teaching, not replace the unique human elements you bring to the classroom.

Start Small

Integration doesn't have to be an all-or-nothing approach. Start small by implementing AI tools in a single lesson or component of your course. This could be as simple as using an AI-powered tool to generate quiz questions or employing a chatbot to help students with homework outside class hours. Small-scale implementations allow you to gauge student response, assess the tool's effectiveness, and make adjustments without overwhelming yourself or your students.

Evaluate, Iterate, and Build

After integrating AI tools on a small scale, evaluate their impact. Ask your students to share their experiences and provide feedback. Did the AI tool help them learn better? Was it accessible to all students? Did it free up your time, enabling you to interact more with learners? Use this feedback to iterate and improve your use of AI in teaching. As you grow more confident and observe positive outcomes, slowly increase AI's role in your curriculum.

Overcoming Challenges

We must recognize the obstacles involved in weaving AI into educational practices. These can include technical issues, training needs, and data privacy concerns. Address these challenges head-on by seeking professional development opportunities, collaborating with IT professionals to ensure a smooth implementation, and being transparent with students and parents about how data is used and protected.

Embracing AI in education offers a pathway to more personalized, engaging, and efficient teaching and learning experiences. By reviewing your curriculum, carefully assessing where AI fits, starting small, and continually evaluating and iterating, you can integrate AI tools into your teaching practices to enhance learning outcomes and support your educational goals.

KEY TAKEAWAYS

- Traditional quizzing methods prioritize memorization over comprehension, limiting long-term retention and catering less to diverse learning styles.
- AI-powered quizzes offer real-time adaptability, providing personalized challenges and immediate feedback to promote deeper understanding.
- AI transforms quizzes into interactive experiences, integrating virtual labs and simulations for practical learning applications.
- Implementing AI in teaching should be gradual, starting with small-scale integration and evaluating impact before expanding further.
- Integrating AI comes with hurdles such as technical glitches, the necessity for training, and worries over data privacy. Addressing these can happen through offering professional development and maintaining open communication.

Just as we explored the transformative power of AI in enhancing personalized learning, our next journey promises to revolutionize how we evaluate progress equally. Building on personalization, we'll see how AI can tailor assessments to each learner's unique path.

CHAPTER 4

AI-INTEGRATION METHOD 3— REVOLUTIONIZING GRADING AND ASSESSMENT

Imagine stepping into a future where AI transforms grading into an adventure. You're about to unlock innovative strategies that seamlessly blend AI with your grading process, making it more efficient and insightful. But, as with all journeys, there are hurdles to overcome, especially in refining grading methods. Let's navigate these challenges together.

THE GRADING DILEMMA

The traditional methods of manual grading present several challenges that impact educators and students alike. Firstly, these methods often fail to consider growth over time and the importance of longitudinal growth, which is crucial for a comprehensive assessment of a student's progress. Here are other issues of manual grading:

- **Subjectivity and biases:** One of the main issues with manual grading is its inherent subjectivity. As a human being, you bring your biases and perspectives to the grading process, which can affect the fairness and consistency of grades. For instance, personal biases may lead to variations in evaluating students' creative or critical thinking skills, which automated systems might overlook due to their focus on predefined criteria.

- **Time-consuming nature:** Manual grading is notoriously time-consuming, particularly for large classes or complex assignments. This extensive time commitment can significantly burden you because you already manage multiple responsibilities. The manual process requires a detailed review of each student's work, which, while allowing for in-depth analysis and personalized feedback, increases the workload on teachers and may lead to teacher burnout or dissatisfaction.

- **Limitations in feedback:** While manual grading allows for personalized feedback, the time constraints and the sheer volume of work often mean that the input may need to be more timely and detailed. This delay can hinder students' ability to learn from their mistakes and improve promptly. Automated grading systems, on the other hand, offer the advantage of providing immediate feedback, allowing for quicker student reflection and adjustment.

Despite these challenges, manual grading has its merits. It enables you to assess qualitative aspects of student work, such as creativity, critical thinking, and depth of understanding, which are often challenging for automated systems to evaluate accurately. Manual grading also allows for a level of personalized feedback that automated systems have yet to match effectively.

How AI Can Help

AI is making a significant impact across various sectors, including education, where it brings many advantages for educators and students. Here's how AI can help, focusing on the topics we've mentioned:

- **Efficiency and timeliness:** AI-powered systems streamline the grading process, significantly reducing the time you spend evaluating exams and assignments. This allows for quicker feedback to students, enhancing their learning experience by enabling timely revisions and understanding of the material.
- **Eliminating bias:** Automated grading systems offer a more objective approach to assessment, reducing the potential for human bias. By following predefined criteria, these systems ensure fair and consistent student evaluations.
- **Accuracy and consistency in grading:** AI algorithms identify patterns and assess responses against predefined standards, ensuring accurate and unbiased grading. This consistency helps maintain fairness and reliability in the assessment process.
- **Adaptive learning and personalized assessments:** AI enables the creation of adaptive learning environments, actively pinpointing each student's strengths and areas for improvement. It then tailors

the learning content and assessments accordingly, providing a personalized learning experience catering to individual educational needs.

- **Tailoring assessments to individual learners:** The ability of AI to process large datasets allows for the customization of learning paths tailored to individual student needs. By identifying students' learning patterns, AI can adapt the difficulty level of quizzes and assignments to challenge them appropriately, fostering a better learning environment.

- **Continuous feedback loops:** AI systems provide real-time feedback to students, highlighting areas that need improvement and offering suggestions for enhancing their learning. This constant feedback loop supports students' educational growth, allowing for immediate adjustments in their study habits and approaches.

The Role of AI in Automated Grading Systems

AI plays a crucial role in the functioning of automated grading systems. Automating grading with AI frees up a significant amount of your time, allowing you to focus more on personal engagement with students and improving their learning experience. Automated grading also offers scalability, enabling the efficient handling of large volumes of assessments. Furthermore, the use of AI in grading goes beyond just efficiency; it encompasses the ability to provide detailed feedback, making educational assessments more meaningful and beneficial for students.

AI-POWERED GRADING SYSTEMS

In today's educational landscape, AI tools are revolutionizing how you approach grading and assessment, making the process more efficient, objective, and scalable. There's an AI tool designed to assist any student assessment, be it exams, essays, or homework. Let's explore some leading AI tools, examine their capabilities, and consider how they can enhance your grading workflow.

Gradescope

Overview and Features

Gradescope streamlines the grading process, especially for handwritten or digital assignments, making it easier and more efficient for educators to evaluate student work. It offers AI-assisted grading, rubric-based evaluation, and detailed analytics to identify areas where students struggle.

Access and Pricing

Available at Gradescope's website. The cost is adjusted according to the size and requirements of each institution.

URL: www.gradescope.com

How to Use It:

- Create an assignment and upload student submissions.
- Set up a detailed rubric.
- Utilize AI to group similar answers and grade them in batches.

- Provide feedback and publish grades.

Prompt Tips

Use detailed rubrics for more effective AI grouping.

Pros and Cons

Pros include time savings and consistency in grading. One con is the initial setup time for detailed rubrics.

Turnitin

Overview and Features

Turnitin is renowned for its ability to detect plagiarism. It also offers grading tools and feedback mechanisms to help you maintain academic integrity and enhance student writing.

Access and Pricing

Available at Turnitin's website. Pricing is institution-based.

URL: www.turnitin.com

How to Use It:

- Assign work through Turnitin.
- Once submitted, Turnitin checks for originality.
- Use the GradeMark feature to provide feedback.
- Review reports and feedback with students.

Prompt Tips

Use Turnitin's comment libraries to streamline feedback.

Pros and Cons

Pros include robust plagiarism detection and valuable writing tools. Cons include potential privacy concerns and the cost for some institutions.

EssayGrader

Overview and Features

EssayGrader is an AI-powered tool designed to grade essays on various criteria, including content relevance, coherence, and grammar.

Access and Pricing

Available at EssayGrader's website. Pricing is subscription-based.

URL: www.essaygrader.ai

How to Use It:

- Upload student essays.
- Configure grading criteria.
- Let AI analyze and grade submissions.
- Review and adjust grades as necessary.

Prompt Tips

Clearly define grading criteria for more accurate AI assessments.

Pros and Cons

Pros include saving time on essay grading and providing detailed feedback. A con is that AI may not fully understand nuances in creative writing.

ZipGrade

Overview and Features

ZipGrade turns your smartphone or tablet into an optical grading machine for multiple-choice tests, offering quick and accurate grading.

Access and Pricing

Available on the App Store and Google Play. Free for limited use, with unlimited scanning plans available for a small fee.

How to Use It:

- Print answer sheets from ZipGrade.
- Administer your test.
- Use the app to scan answer sheets.
- Instantly view grades and analytics.

Prompt Tips

This detail isn't applicable, given the nature of the tool.

Pros and Cons

Pros include instant grading and analysis, but it's limited to multiple-choice formats.

Canvas

Overview and Features

Canvas is a comprehensive educational platform with grading, assessments, course management, and more features. Its grading tools are integrated within a larger ecosystem to facilitate online learning.

Access and Pricing

Available at Canvas's website. Pricing varies.

URL: www.instructure.com/canvas

How to Use It:

- Set up your course and assignments in Canvas.
- Students submit work through the platform.
- Grade submissions using Canvas's SpeedGrader.
- Provide feedback and publish grades directly to students.

Prompt Tips

Utilize Canvas's rubric feature for consistent grading.

Pros and Cons

Pros include a comprehensive suite of tools beyond grading. New users might need help with the learning curve.

General Steps for Using AI Grading Tools

- Select the tool that aligns best with your specific needs and the subject you're teaching.

- Set up your class and assignments according to the tool's guidelines.
- Familiarize yourself with the tool's AI capabilities and how it integrates with your teaching style.
- Continuously adjust grading parameters based on student performance.

BALANCING AUTOMATION WITH PERSONALIZED FEEDBACK

In today's quickly changing educational and professional development landscape, finding ways to make processes more efficient while maintaining a personal touch is more important than ever. As you seek to optimize efficiency through automation, it's vital to remember the unparalleled value of personalized human feedback. Maintaining this equilibrium is crucial for its benefits and as a foundational element in nurturing profound learning and active participation. Let's explore how to strike the perfect equilibrium, ensuring that your automated systems enhance rather than diminish the learning experience.

Importance of Balancing Automation with Personalized Feedback

- **Human touch in a digital world:** Despite the efficiency of automated grading systems in handling multiple-choice and fill-in-the-blank questions, they need to improve in assessing complex assignments like essays or projects that require creativity and critical thinking. Here, personalized feedback becomes irreplaceable, offering insights that algorithms cannot replicate.

It's about adding a human touch to the digital experience, recognizing efforts, and guiding improvements to foster a deeper connection and understanding.

- **Enhanced learning experience:** Research indicates that personalized feedback significantly impacts learners' motivation and ability to improve. For instance, a Journal of Educational Psychology study found that detailed, customized feedback led to better student performance than generic comments or grades alone (Butler, 1988). This suggests that while automation can streamline the grading process, incorporating human feedback can elevate the learning experience, making it more meaningful and impactful.

- **Emotional and cognitive engagement:** Personalized feedback enhances the intellectual dimensions of learning and touches upon the emotional layers, influencing how learners feel and engage with the material. It shows learners that their work is valued and that there's a genuine interest in their success. This emotional engagement is crucial for motivation, persistence, and developing a growth mindset.

Tips and Strategies for Finding Balance

Balancing automation with personalized feedback in educational environments is critical for fostering effective learning and engagement. As you delve into teaching or educational technology, finding the proper equilibrium between leveraging automation for efficiency and providing personalized, human feedback for depth and understanding can be a game-changer. Here's a guide to help you navigate this balance, ensuring your students reap both worlds' benefits.

Understanding the Importance of Balance

Firstly, it's essential to recognize why striking this balance is crucial. Automated grading systems, powered by sophisticated algorithms, can efficiently handle repetitive tasks, such as multiple-choice questions or factual/false statements, saving you significant time. However, these systems cannot understand the nuances of a student's thought process or provide constructive criticism and encouragement that can only come from a human. On the other hand, personalized feedback addresses these limitations by offering tailored guidance, fostering a deeper understanding, and encouraging critical thinking and growth.

Strategies for Finding Balance

- **Use automation for initial assessments:** Start using automated tools for straightforward assessments. This approach allows you to quickly identify areas where students perform well and where they struggle without consuming too much of your time.
- **Provide personalized feedback on complex assignments:** For essays, projects, or complex problem-solving tasks, personalized feedback is indispensable. Use the insights from automated assessments to focus your personalized input on areas that need the most attention, making your comments more impactful.
- **Employ tools that offer customizable feedback options:** Some educational technology tools allow

for a blend of automated and personalized feedback. These tools can automatically grade assignments based on criteria you set while also providing the option to add customized comments or video feedback, bringing a human touch to the automated process.

- **Schedule regular one-on-one sessions:** Regularly scheduled one-on-one sessions with your students can complement the automated feedback system. Use these sessions to discuss the computerized feedback, delve deeper into the student's learning process, and offer personalized guidance and support.
- **Continuous learning and adaptation:** Keep up with the latest educational technology and teaching trends by actively participating in workshops, webinars, and conferences. Engage with professional learning communities to exchange ideas and innovations in education. This continuous learning will help you refine your approach to balancing automation with personalized feedback, ensuring it remains effective and responsive to your student's needs.

Examples and Practical Applications

Consider a scenario where you use an automated system to grade multiple-choice quizzes every week. The system reveals that many students are having difficulty grasping a specific concept. You then review these results and dedicate part of the next class to re-explain the concept, using examples tailored to the student's interests and previous work. Additionally, you provide personalized written feedback on a recent essay assignment, highlighting strengths, areas for improvement, and strategies for advancement.

Another example is an online course instructor who uses a platform that integrates automated grading with the ability to insert personalized video feedback. The instructor sends short, personalized video messages to students who performed exceptionally well or poorly in the computerized assessments, offering encouragement, insights into their performance, and tips for improvement.

Balancing automation with personalized feedback is not just about finding the right tools but also about adopting a mindset that values the unique contributions of both technology and human insight. Embracing this equilibrium allows you to foster a learning environment that's more engaging and effective but also adaptable to the varied needs of your students, ensuring a comprehensive educational experience. Remember, the goal is to enhance learning outcomes, foster personal growth, and prepare students for the challenges ahead, all while managing your workload effectively.

Incorporate these strategies and tips into your teaching practices, and witness the transformative impact of a well-balanced approach to feedback on your student's educational journey.

IMPLEMENTATION GUIDE FOR METHOD 3

Integrating AI into the grading and assessment of student work can significantly enhance the efficiency and effectiveness of educational practices. However, transitioning to such a system requires careful planning and consideration. Here are practical tips and guidelines to help you smoothly incorporate AI interventions into your routines, ensuring a blend of technological innovation and educational integrity.

Assess Where AI Should and Shouldn't Be Implemented

Begin by evaluating the areas within your grading system that could benefit most from AI assistance. AI tools are particularly adept at handling repetitive, time-consuming tasks such as grading quizzes, standardized tests, or multiple-choice questions. However, they might still need to be fully capable of assessing more subjective assignments like essays or creative projects with the same nuance a human teacher can. Identifying the balance between AI's efficiency and human insight is crucial. For example, use AI to handle the bulk of objective grading, freeing up your time to evaluate more complex student work personally.

Choose the Right AI Tools

Choose AI grading tools that best fit your teaching subjects and needs. Look for those with a strong reputation for accuracy and reliability in educational environments. Consider features like ease of integration with existing systems, support for various question types, and the ability to provide meaningful feedback to students. You can widely adopt platforms like Turnitin and Gradescope for their versatility in managing multiple types of assessments and their strong performance.

Start Small

Integrating AI into your grading process doesn't mean an overnight overhaul. Start with a pilot program by automating the grading of quizzes or other straightforward tasks. This approach allows you to gauge the effectiveness of the AI tool, identify any issues early on, and make adjustments without disrupting your entire grading system. This also helps you become familiar with the technology, grasping what it can do and its limits.

Train the AI for Grading Tasks

Many AI grading tools use machine learning algorithms that improve with training. Spend time upfront training the AI on your specific grading criteria. This might involve feeding it examples of graded assignments so it can learn from your grading style. The more data the AI has, the better it can mimic your grading nuances, leading to more accurate and consistent grading. This step is crucial for assignments that require a degree of subjective judgment.

Evaluate, Iterate, and Build

After implementing AI grading, continuously monitor its performance and impact on your workload and the student's learning experience. Collect feedback from students to understand how the AI-generated feedback influences their learning. Leverage this feedback to refine and enhance the system continuously through iterative updates. Remember, integrating AI into grading is not a set-it-and-forget-it solution; it's a dynamic process that evolves with your teaching practices and the needs of your students.

Incorporating AI into the grading and assessment process offers numerous benefits, including increased efficiency and the ability to provide instant feedback to students—the effectiveness of integrating AI hinges on careful planning and continuous assessment. By starting small, choosing the right tools, and continuously refining the process, you can harness the power of AI to enhance your teaching practice without losing the personal touch that is so critical to effective education.

Embrace AI as a partner in the educational process, one that can handle specific tasks while you focus on the more nuanced aspects of teaching and learning. With careful planning and an open mind, AI can become an invaluable asset in your educational toolkit, improving outcomes for you and your students.

KEY TAKEAWAYS

- Traditional manual grading often overlooks longitudinal growth, is subject to biases, is time-consuming, and may provide limited feedback.
- AI can enhance grading efficiency, reduce bias, and ensure accuracy and consistency while enabling adaptive learning and personalized assessments.
- Start integrating AI by assessing where it's most beneficial, choosing the right tools, starting small, training AI on grading tasks, and continuously evaluating and iterating the process.

- Balancing automated grading with personalized feedback is essential for a meaningful learning experience and maintaining the human touch in digital education.
- Implementing AI in grading should begin with identifying tasks suited for automation, selecting appropriate tools, starting with pilot programs, training AI with specific grading criteria, and continuously monitoring and refining the process.

Having explored how AI can revolutionize grading and assessment, enhancing efficiency and personalizing feedback, you're now ready to research new teaching materials and methods. This journey will seamlessly blend the insights gained from AI in grading with innovative approaches to curriculum development and instructional strategies, promising a comprehensive transformation in your teaching experience.

MAKE A DIFFERENCE WITH YOUR REVIEW

UNLOCK THE POWER OF UNDERSTANDING

"Intelligence plus character—that is the goal of true education."

DR. MARTIN LUTHER KING JR.

This profound statement underscores the essence of what we strive for in the educational realm. It is in this spirit of generosity and collective uplifting that I reach out to you today.

My collective goal is to make the insights and strategies within "Integrating AI in the Classroom" universally accessible, empowering educators at every level to revolutionize their teaching methodologies. Achieving this ambitious vision, however, requires reaching an audience as broad and diverse as the educational community itself.

This is where your invaluable contribution comes into play. The influence of your review cannot be overstated; it serves as a beacon for countless educators navigating the vast sea of resources in search of reliable and transformative tools.

By sharing your thoughts and experiences about "Integrating AI in the Classroom," you're not just critiquing a book; you're lighting a path for gifted teachers to better serve their students.

If this book has sparked a flame of inspiration within you, I encourage you to share it.

Simply scan the QR code or follow the link to leave your review:

https://www.amazon.com/review/create-review/?
asin=B0D3Q7NKJS

I eagerly look forward to sharing with you more of the insights and strategies that "Integrating AI in the Classroom" has to offer.

With the deepest gratitude, - JH Madron

CHAPTER 5
AI-INTEGRATION METHOD 4— RESEARCHING NEW TEACHING MATERIALS AND METHODS

From chalkboards to digital tablets, the journey of educational methodologies has been quite remarkable. AI now leads the charge, transforming the way we teach and learn. UNESCO underscores AI's potential to tackle significant academic challenges, innovate learning practices, and accelerate progress toward inclusive and equitable education (*Artificial Intelligence*, n.d.).

By fostering a human-centered approach, UNESCO aims to ensure AI benefits all, bridging the digital divide rather than widening it. It's about making AI work for everyone, turning technological advances into accessible innovations and knowledge for all. This vision is encapsulated in initiatives like the Beijing Consensus, guiding policymakers to harness AI's potential responsibly (*Artificial Intelligence*, n.d.).

HOW AI CAN HELP WITH RESEARCH

You face significant challenges when relying on traditional methods to research teaching materials and methods. These challenges include limitations in time, resources, and the accessibility of relevant information, which can hinder the effectiveness and innovation of teaching practices.

Traditional methods primarily use printed textbooks, academic journals, and the expertise of educators. This approach can be time-consuming and must consistently provide the most current or diverse perspectives on teaching strategies. For instance, if you're new to the field, you typically learn through instruction in college settings and practicums under experienced teachers. This approach can lead to the persistence of outdated practices, as you might stick with the methods taught despite newer research indicating more effective strategies.

Moreover, traditional methods can limit access to innovative teaching materials and methods. You may need help finding resources catering to diverse learning needs or incorporating the latest technological advancements in education. This is particularly challenging in subjects like mathematics, where integrating technology can significantly enhance teaching and learning. Traditional teaching methods frequently overlook digital tools that can offer dynamic and interactive learning experiences. Increasingly, educators recognize these tools as crucial for captivating students and adapting to diverse learning styles.

In contrast, AI-driven recommendation systems and tools for educational content offer a promising solution to these challenges. These technologies can analyze vast amounts of data to generate and customize teaching materials based on individual teaching styles and student needs. AI can help you discover the most relevant, effective, and up-to-date teaching strategies and materials tailored to their specific classroom dynamics.

For example, adaptive learning technologies can personalize educational content for students, ensuring that materials are suited to their unique learning pace and style. This can lead to more effective learning outcomes by addressing students' individual needs, a strategy that traditional methods often fail to achieve due to their one-size-fits-all approach. Furthermore, AI can assist in identifying gaps in students' understanding, allowing you to adjust your teaching strategies in real time to address these issues.

AI-driven tools also offer the potential to save you significant time in planning and researching teaching materials. Instead of sifting through countless books and articles, you can rely on AI systems to recommend the most relevant resources based on the latest research and trends in education. This approach allows you to dedicate more time to engaging with your students and honing your teaching methods.

AI-DRIVEN CONTENT CURATION

Given the vast landscape of AI tools available today, it's no surprise that you seek the most effective resources to enhance teaching and learning experiences. AI tools can significantly streamline curating and recommending teaching materials that match your teaching style and cater to your student's learning preferences. Here's a curated list of AI tools that stand out for their capabilities in assisting you:

Google Scholar

- **Overview:** Google Scholar, a free web search engine, indexes the full text or metadata of scholarly literature across various publishing formats and disciplines.
- **Access and pricing:** Available at Google Scholar. It's free.
- **URL:** scholar.google.com/.
- **Usage guide:** Use keywords related to your teaching subject to find articles, theses, books, and conference papers. Adjust your alerts to keep abreast of the newest research developments.
- **Customization for teaching:** Filter results by year to get the most recent studies or use the "cited by" feature to find influential papers.
- **Pros and cons:** Pros include comprehensive access to academic resources. One con is the potential for overwhelming amounts of information.

Scite

- **Overview:** Scite, an AI-powered tool, revolutionizes how researchers discover and comprehend scientific articles by utilizing Smart Citations to enhance their search and understanding.
- **Access and pricing:** Available at Scite. Offers both free and premium subscription models.

- **URL:** www.scite.ai
- **Usage guide:** Search for articles and view how they have been cited (supporting, contrasting, or mentioning), providing insight into the paper's impact.
- **Customization for teaching:** Use the citation context to find materials that align with your teaching perspective.
- **Pros and cons:** Pros include insightful analysis of paper impact. Cons include the limited depth of its database compared to more extensive indexes.

Trinka

- **Overview:** Trinka is an AI-powered tool for academic and technical writing.
- **Access and pricing:** Available at Trinka. There's a free basic version. Premium plans offer more features. **URL:** www.trinka.ai
- **Usage guide:** Upload your teaching materials or drafts to get grammar, tone, and style suggestions.
- **Customization for teaching:** Tailor feedback settings to suit academic writing standards or specific disciplines.
- **Pros and cons:** The pro is its focus on academic and technical writing. A con is that advanced features require a subscription.

Elicit

- **Overview:** Elicit is a research assistant that uses AI to help you find papers relevant to your query.

- **Access and pricing:** You must sign up at Elicit. Currently in beta and free to use.
- **URL:** elicit.org
- **Usage guide:** Enter a research question, and Elicit suggests relevant papers and provides summaries.
- **Customization for teaching:** Use it to find cutting-edge research tailored to your curriculum needs.
- **Pros and cons:** Pros include efficient research paper discovery and summaries. The main con is that it's still in development, which might limit some features.

Scholarcy

- **Overview:** Scholarcy is an AI tool that reads research papers, reports, and book chapters, creating an interactive summary with key findings and references.
- **Access and pricing:** Available at Scholarcy. It offers a free trial, but you must choose from subscription options for continued use.
- **URL:** www.scholarcy.com
- **Usage guide:** Upload a document to get a concise summary, key points, and links to cited sources.
- **Customization for teaching:** Generate summaries for a quick overview or to decide on relevance for your curriculum.
- **Pros and cons:** Pros include time-saving summaries and easy extraction of critical points. Cons involve subscription costs for full features.

Additional Notable Mentions

- Knewton and IBM Watson deliver personalized learning experiences by leveraging adaptive learning technologies.
- Tableau and Consensus provide data visualization and decision-making tools that help interpret student performance data.
- MagicSchool.ai, Bing Chat, and ChatGPT can offer interactive learning experiences and content creation assistance.
- Perplexity, Diffit, Education Copilot, Nolej, Eduaide.ai, Summarize.tech, and Parlay Genie are emerging tools focusing on various aspects of educational support, from tutoring assistance to content summarization and discussion facilitation.

Consider the unique requirements of your curriculum and teaching style when selecting AI tools. Many of these tools offer customization options to align with your educational goals, whether through setting preferences, filtering options, or specifying search queries.

Here are some essential guidelines for incorporating these AI tools into your instructional methods:

- **Start small:** Start by incorporating one tool at a time to discover the perfect match for your teaching approach and the unique learning requirements of your students.
- **Seek feedback:** Regularly ask your students for

feedback on the effectiveness of your tools and materials.

- **Stay updated:** AI and educational technology evolves rapidly. Keep an eye on updates and new tools that enhance your teaching.

Remember that the aim is to enrich the learning journey to avoid burdening yourself or your students with too much technology. The right AI tools can provide powerful support, helping you to curate and recommend relevant teaching materials efficiently and effectively.

TURNING RESEARCH INTO ENGAGING LESSONS

Creating engaging and interactive lessons and presentations from new teaching materials and methods can be formidable. Many AI tools are available to help transform your content into captivating educational experiences. Here's a guide to some of the most relevant AI tools, including an overview, where to access them, pricing, a step-by-step usage guide, prompt tips, and their pros and cons. This guide is designed with you in mind, aiming to support you in leveraging the latest technology to enrich your teaching.

Canva Magic Write

- **Overview and features:** Canva Magic Write is an AI-powered tool designed to assist in creating visually appealing presentations and educational materials. It offers features for generating text content, designing layouts, and selecting templates.

- **Access and pricing:** Available through the Canva platform. The free version is available; the pro version offers additional features.
- **URL:** canva.com
- **How to use it:** Select a template, then use Magic Write to generate content or improve your text. Customize the design to suit your lesson.
- **Prompt tips:** Be specific about your topic and intended audience for more tailored content.
- **Pros and cons:** User-friendly; integrates text and design seamlessly. Limited control over creative aspects in the free version.

Beautiful AI

- **Overview and features:** Beautiful AI focuses on creating professional-looking presentations with innovative templates that adapt to your content.
- **Access and pricing:** www.beautiful.ai offers a free plan; premium plans provide more features.
- **How to use it:** Choose a template and start adding your content. The AI automatically adjusts the layout.
- **Pros and cons:** Saves time with auto-adjusting layouts; intuitive interface. On the other hand, there's less flexibility for manual design adjustments.

SlidesAI.io

- **Overview and features:** This tool uses AI to help design slides based on text input, making it easier to create presentations.
- **Access and pricing:** www.slidesai.io. Free access with limited features; subscription plans available.
- **How to use it:** Input your lecture notes or outlines, and let SlidesAI generate a presentation.
- **Pros and cons:** Streamlines slide creation; suitable for quick presentations. It may require adjustments for specific design preferences.

PowerPoint Speaker Coach

- **Overview and features:** An AI feature within PowerPoint that offers real-time feedback on your presentation skills.
- **Access and pricing:** Available in Microsoft PowerPoint. Part of Microsoft Office Suite.
- **How to use it:** Start rehearsing your presentation with Speaker Coach enabled to receive feedback.
- **Pros and cons:** Improves public speaking skills; feedback on pacing, filler words, etc. Feedback may only cover some nuances of effective speaking.

Adobe Express With Firefly

- **Overview and features:** Adobe Express now includes Firefly, Adobe's AI for creating graphics, video, and web pages quickly.

- **Access and pricing:** Adobe Express website. The starter plan is free, but subscribing is necessary to access premium features.
- **How to use it:** Choose the type of content you want to create and use Firefly to assist in the design process.
- **Pros and cons:** Pros include versatile content creation and an extensive asset library. New users often face a learning curve.

Bing Image Creator

- **Overview and features:** An AI-powered tool by Microsoft that generates images based on text descriptions.
- **Access and pricing:** Through Bing search engine. Free to use.
- **How to use it:** Enter a descriptive prompt to create images for your educational content.
- **Pros and cons:** Quick image creation; can generate unique visuals. Images may sometimes need to match the desired outcome perfectly.

Pictory

- **Overview and features:** Pictory employs AI technology to convert text content into captivating video presentations.
- **Access and pricing:** www.pictory.ai. A free trial is available; subscription plans are available for more features.

- **How to use it:** Upload your text, and Pictory converts it into a customized storyboard.
- **Pros and cons:** Makes video content creation accessible; supports various formats. Subscription plans can be pricey for full features.

Curipod

- **Overview and features:** An AI-based platform designed for you to create interactive and personalized learning experiences.
- **Access and pricing:** curipod.com. A free version and premium plans are available.
- **How to use it:** Use the platform to build lessons with interactive elements like quizzes and videos.
- **Pros and cons:** Focuses on engagement and interactivity; easy to integrate with existing materials. It may require time to explore and utilize all features fully.

Simplified

- **Overview and features:** Simplified offers AI-driven design, video, and copywriting tools to create content for educational purposes.
- **Access and pricing:** simplified.co. A free version is available; additional features require a subscription.
- **How to use it:** Select the type of content you want to create and use the AI tools to assist in the creation process.
- **Pros and cons:** It offers an all-in-one platform for

content types and intuitive design. Premium features necessitate a subscription.

Slidebean

- **Overview and features:** Slidebean streamlines the presentation design process, enabling users to concentrate on their content.
- **Access and pricing:** slidebean.com. Free trial; subscription plans for more features.
- **How to use it:** Input your content, and Slidebean designs your presentation.
- **Pros and cons:** Saves time on design; professional-looking presentations. Less control over the design process.

Every tool brings its own set of distinctive features to the table, enabling you to craft lessons and presentations that are more engaging and interactive. Experiment with them to discover which best suits your teaching style and material. Remember, the goal is to enhance learning outcomes and make the educational process more enjoyable and effective for your students.

IMPLEMENTATION GUIDE FOR METHOD 4

Embarking on integrating AI into your research practices is akin to navigating the vast expanse of the digital age's frontier. It's an adventure filled with innovation, efficiency, and discovery opportunities. However, like any expedition into unknown territory, it requires preparation, strategy, and an open mind. Let's explore how you can seamlessly blend AI into your existing research methodologies, ensuring you leverage its potential to enhance learning outcomes and student engagement.

Review Your Curriculum

Firstly, take a moment to review your curriculum thoroughly. Identifying these areas is critical, allowing you to pinpoint where AI can deliver the most substantial benefits. For instance, are there complex data analysis tasks that AI could streamline? What are the areas where content generated by AI could make learning experiences more captivating for students? By pinpointing these opportunities, you're laying the groundwork for a more informed and strategic integration of AI tools.

Assess Where AI Should and Shouldn't Be Implemented

Not all aspects of your curriculum will benefit from AI integration. It's essential to critically assess where its application will be genuinely beneficial and where it might not add value or potentially detract from the learning experience. For example, while AI can be invaluable in analyzing large data sets, it may not be suitable for teaching soft skills, such as critical thinking or ethical reasoning, where human interaction and discussion are essential. Making these distinctions early on will save you time and ensure that AI enhances rather than hinders your curriculum.

Start Small

When integrating AI into your research practices, starting small is wise. Choose a single course or module where you believe AI can make a significant impact, and pilot your ideas there. This approach allows you to manage the transition more effectively, troubleshoot issues, and gauge student response without overwhelming yourself or your students. An example could be implementing an AI tool that helps students analyze research data more efficiently, giving them more time to focus on interpretation and discussion.

Evaluate, Iterate, and Build

This step is where the magic happens. Understanding the impact of AI on your teaching and your student's learning is crucial, and evaluation plays a vital role in this process. After implementing AI tools or methods, closely monitor how they affect student engagement and learning outcomes. Are students more engaged? Do they understand concepts more deeply? Gather data through surveys, feedback sessions, and analyzing performance metrics.

Keep going! Use this feedback to refine and enhance your AI integration efforts. Maybe you need to adjust the tool to fit your students' needs better, or they may use it in ways you didn't initially expect. This iterative process is crucial for refining the role of AI in your curriculum and ensuring that it serves your educational goals effectively.

The Importance of Evaluating the Impact

Evaluating the impact of AI-enhanced teaching materials and methods cannot be overstated. The focus isn't solely on the functionality of technology; it's on its ability to enhance the learning journey. For example, imagine introducing an AI tool designed to assist students in mastering statistical analysis. In that case, the measure of success isn't just whether the tool functions but whether students' understanding of statistical analysis improves.

Assessing the impact based on student engagement and learning outcomes provides concrete evidence of the value AI brings to your teaching. It also helps in making the case for broader implementation across your institution. Remember, the ultimate goal of integrating AI into research practices is to facilitate a richer, more engaging learning experience that prepares students for the challenges of the modern world.

Incorporating AI into your research methods opens up exciting possibilities to improve educational results and captivate students innovatively. By reviewing your curriculum, assessing where AI fits best, starting small, and rigorously evaluating the impact, you can confidently navigate the complexities of this integration process.

KEY TAKEAWAYS

- Traditional research methods in education can be time-consuming and may only sometimes reflect the most current or diverse perspectives.

- AI-driven tools can customize teaching materials based on individual teaching styles and student needs, offering a solution to the limitations of traditional methods.
- Adaptive learning technologies enable personalized educational content for students, improving learning outcomes by catering to individual needs.
- AI can save you significant time planning and researching teaching materials by recommending relevant resources based on the latest research and trends.
- You are encouraged to start small when integrating AI into your practices, assess its impact carefully, and use student feedback to iterate and improve AI integration.
- Evaluating the impact of AI on teaching and learning is crucial, with a focus on how it affects student engagement and understanding.

In exploring how AI can enhance group learning, we've seen its power in personalizing education. Now, let's explore how integrating AI can offer personalized support to each student. This approach deepens our journey, seamlessly connecting the dots between collaborative learning and tailoring individual student experiences. You're meticulously guiding every learner with attention and compassion.

CHAPTER 6

AI-INTEGRATION METHOD 5—PROVIDING ONE-TO-ONE SUPPORT FOR STUDENTS

Envision stepping into a classroom where each student's learning journey is as distinct as their fingerprint. In this dynamic setting, you face the universal challenge: engaging with a curriculum that often feels one-size-fits-all, leaving many students disengaged and struggling to keep pace. AI is a shining example of personalized learning that revolutionizes education by tailoring learning experiences to your needs, interests, and pace, offering adaptive content, interactive experiences, and insightful data analysis to optimize learning outcomes. Research indicates that many students disengage from their learning due to uninteresting, inflexible curriculums (*Why Your Students*, 2022).

AI's capability to adapt educational content dynamically ensures that learning is relevant, engaging, and aligned with each student's aspirations, boosting interest and involvement.

ADDRESSING DIVERSE LEARNING NEEDS IN THE CLASSROOM USING AI

The educational landscape is transforming, and at the heart of this transformation is the shift toward inclusive education —a model that recognizes and values the diversity of student populations along with their unique learning needs and abilities. As an educator, you must acknowledge the broad spectrum of differences in learning styles, strengths, and challenges that students bring to the classroom. The ultimate goal? To provide an equitable educational experience that supports every student's success. But how do we tackle the challenge of meeting such a wide array of needs in a practical, scalable way? Enter AI.

The Role of AI in Fostering Inclusive Education

AI technology can be a game-changer in creating more inclusive educational environments. It offers tools and solutions that can adapt to students' individual learning needs, making personalized education not just an aspiration but a reality. Here's how AI can help:

- **Timely, specific feedback:** The traditional feedback model often needs to catch up due to time constraints and the sheer impracticality of delivering personalized feedback at scale. AI can fill this gap by offering timely, specific feedback to students, which is crucial for their learning and development. This is not about replacing the invaluable human touch in education but augmenting it with technology that can provide instant feedback on assignments or practice work, identify errors, and offer corrections or suggestions for improvement.

- **Personalized learning paths:** AI tutoring systems and learning platforms can analyze how students interact with the material, identifying patterns, strengths, and weaknesses in their learning. This data can tailor learning content, adjust difficulty levels, and suggest resources that meet each student's needs. Imagine a scenario where one student receives additional practice problems in algebra because the system has identified a challenging area. At the same time, another is guided toward more advanced reading materials, pushing their comprehension skills further.

- **Engagement and motivation:** By tailoring learning experiences to individual interests and learning styles, AI can help increase student engagement and motivation. For example, students who find math challenging could engage with problem sets framed within contexts that captivate them, like sports statistics or video game coding, making their learning journey more exciting and tailored to their passions.

Tips for Utilizing AI to Enhance Learning

How can you leverage AI to tailor activities to students' strengths and weaknesses? Here are some practical tips:

- **Incorporate AI-based assessment tools:** Use AI-driven assessment tools to gain insights into your students' learning patterns and knowledge gaps.

These tools can provide detailed reports on each student's performance, helping you to customize your teaching strategies accordingly.

- **Adopt AI tutoring systems:** Integrate AI tutoring systems into your classroom activities. These systems can offer students personalized instruction and practice opportunities, allowing them to work independently and receive immediate feedback.
- **Utilize AI for differentiated learning:** AI can help you design differentiated learning activities that cater to the varied needs of your students. By analyzing student learning preferences and performance data, AI tools can suggest activities, resources, and projects tailored to different learning styles and abilities.
- **Engage students with interactive AI tools:** Leverage interactive AI tools that can make learning more engaging for students. Whether through educational games, simulations, or virtual reality experiences, these tools can provide immersive learning experiences that cater to diverse learning preferences.
- **Foster collaborative learning with AI:** Use AI to facilitate collaborative projects where students with different strengths and weaknesses can work together, learn from each other, and achieve common goals. AI can help match students with complementary skills or suggest roles within a project based on their proficiencies.

The Future Is Now

The journey toward fully inclusive education is ongoing, and while challenges remain, the potential of AI to support this goal is immense. By leveraging AI, you can provide personalized, engaging, and effective learning experiences that recognize and celebrate the diversity of student needs and abilities. It's not just about integrating new technologies into the classroom; it's about rethinking the approach to education to ensure that every student has the opportunity to succeed.

Moving forward, you must keep up with the newest AI advancements and discover ways to apply these technologies to improve learning outcomes. The future of education is inclusive, and with AI, that future is within reach.

Remember, the goal of inclusive education is not to apply a one-size-fits-all solution but to create a flexible and responsive learning environment that adapts to the needs of each student. AI offers the tools and capabilities to make this vision a reality, transforming how we teach and learn for the better. So, let's embrace the possibilities and work toward an educational system where every student can thrive regardless of their background, abilities, or learning styles.

AI-POWERED ADAPTIVE LEARNING PLATFORMS AND TOOLS

In the dynamic landscape of education, leveraging AI platforms and tools can significantly enhance student learning outcomes. These AI-driven solutions are adept at adapting to diverse student needs, offering personalized learning experiences that cater to individual learning styles, paces, and preferences.

Squirrel AI

- **Overview and features:** Squirrel AI leads personalized learning using an advanced adaptive learning algorithm to customize content according to each student's unique needs and pace. It identifies knowledge gaps and delivers targeted lessons that suit the learner's current level and learning style.
- **Access and pricing:** Available online through their website or mobile application. Offers a subscription model; specific pricing details may vary, so it's advisable to check their website for the most current information.
- **Usage guide:** Sign up, input student learning goals, and let the AI assess the student's current knowledge level. The platform then guides the student through personalized learning paths.
- **Prompt tips:** Encourage students to engage regularly and honestly with the assessments for optimal personalization.
- **Pros and cons:** Offers deep personalization but may require time for students to adapt to the learning model.

IBM Watson Classroom

- **Overview and features:** IBM Watson Classroom leverages cognitive computing to enhance educational experiences, offering insights into students' learning preferences and potential areas for improvement. It supports you in creating more engaging and effective learning environments.

- **Access and pricing:** Available through IBM's education solutions portal. Custom pricing based on institution needs.
- **Usage guide:** You input student data, and Watson provides analytics and insights for personalized learning experiences.
- **Prompt tips:** Utilize Watson's insights to tailor classroom discussions, activities, and assignments.
- **Pros and cons:** Highly sophisticated analytics tool with a steep learning curve for optimal utilization.

Copilot Education

- **Overview and features:** This AI tool helps create engaging, interactive educational content, making the learning experience more dynamic for students. It allows you to integrate multimedia resources into your lessons effortlessly.
- **Access and pricing:** Available on their platform, they provide various pricing levels, including a free tier with limited features.
- **Usage guide:** Sign up, choose a template, or start from scratch and use the intuitive editor to create engaging lessons.
- **Prompt tips:** Explore various media types to discover which most effectively boosts student engagement.
- **Pros and cons:** Easy content creation with potential

limitations in the free version regarding feature access.

Classpoint AI

- **Overview and features:** Classpoint AI is an interactive teaching tool that integrates with PowerPoint to transform presentations into interactive learning experiences, enabling real-time feedback and assessments.
- **Access and pricing:** Downloadable add-on for PowerPoint. A free tier is available; premium features require a subscription.
- **Usage guide:** Install Classpoint, open PowerPoint, and create interactive slides engaging students.
- **Prompt tips:** Use interactive quizzes and polls to measure student understanding in real time.
- **Pros and cons:** Enhances engagement through presentations; reliance on PowerPoint may only suit some teaching styles.

Fobizz

- **Overview and features:** Fobizz offers a platform for teachers' professional development, focusing on integrating digital tools and AI in teaching. It provides courses and resources to help you upskill.
- **Access and pricing:** You must register on their website, and the requirements vary depending on the course and access level.
- **Usage guide:** Choose a course, participate in

interactive sessions, and apply your learning to your teaching practice.

- **Pros and cons:** Great for professional development; course selection may be limited by specific interests or needs.

Teddy AI

- **Overview and features:** Teddy AI specializes in early education, offering a friendly AI companion that engages children in interactive learning activities tailored to their developmental stage.
- **Access and pricing:** The mobile app is available on various platforms. Subscription-based, with options for different levels of access.
- **Usage guide:** Download the app, set up a profile for your child, and let Teddy guide them through learning adventures.
- **Pros and cons:** Engages young learners effectively; content is mainly for early education stages.

EdApp

- **Overview and features:** EdApp is a mobile learning management system that uses microlearning and gamification to deliver bite-sized, engaging learning experiences suitable for corporate training and education.
- **Access and pricing:** Mobile and web platforms offer a free version while providing premium features through a subscription.

- **Usage guide:** Sign up, create or select courses, and deploy to learners. Utilize analytics to track progress.
- **Prompt tips:** Leverage gamification features to increase learner motivation and retention.
- **Pros and cons:** Effective microlearning platform; might require creative setup for traditional educational settings.

Adaptemy

- **Overview and features:** Adaptemy delivers adaptive learning solutions for publishers and schools, offering customizable curricula that adapt to student performance and engagement in real time.
- **Access and pricing:** Web-based platform. Custom pricing based on implementation scale and needs.
- **Usage guide:** Collaborate with Adaptemy to integrate their technology with your curriculum, then monitor and adjust as needed based on analytics.
- **Pros and cons:** Highly customizable; implementation may require significant upfront planning.

CogBooks

- **Overview and features:** CogBooks is an advanced adaptive learning platform that personalizes the learning experience for higher education students, adapting content and assessments to fit their learning needs.

- **Access and pricing:** Online platform. Institution-based pricing.
- **Usage guide:** Institutions partner with CogBooks to implement adaptive learning in their courses, leveraging the platform's analytics to improve outcomes.
- **Pros and cons:** Supports higher education effectively; may not be accessible for individual educators.

Smart Sparrow

- **Overview and features:** Smart Sparrow is an adaptive eLearning platform that allows you to create rich, interactive, and adaptive learning experiences, focusing on science and health education.
- **Access and pricing:** Online platform. Pricing varies; contact for details.
- **Usage guide:** Use the platform to design and deploy adaptive learning experiences, utilizing analytics to refine and improve content.
- **Pros and cons:** Powerful for creating interactive content; focus on specific subject areas may limit applicability.

Pearson Interactive Labs

- **Overview and features:** Pearson offers interactive labs that utilize AI to provide immersive learning experiences in various subjects, enhancing understanding through interactive simulations and activities.

- **Access and pricing:** Availability on Pearson's platform varies based on the course and agreements with the institution.
- **Usage guide:** Integrated into Pearson's curriculum offerings, you can incorporate labs into their teaching materials.
- **Pros and cons:** Enhances learning with simulations; availability may depend on institutional subscriptions.

Impelsys Scholar ALS

- **Overview and features:** This AI-driven learning solution focuses on higher education and professional training, offering a platform that supports adaptive learning strategies to improve learning outcomes.
- **Access and pricing:** Web-based service. Custom pricing model.
- **Usage guide:** Partner with Impelsys to integrate the platform into your educational offerings, then utilize its features to enhance learning.
- **Pros and cons:** Suitable for higher education and professional training; may require institutional commitment for full benefits.

Knewton

- **Overview and features:** Knewton provides an adaptive learning platform that personalizes educational content, making learning more efficient and effective by adapting to the learner's pace and performance.
- **Access and pricing:** The online platform provides different pricing models based on how you implement it.
- **Usage guide:** Integrate Knewton with your existing course materials to provide adaptive learning paths for students.
- **Pros and cons:** Offers robust adaptivity; effectiveness depends on the integration quality with course materials.

In integrating these AI tools into your educational practice, consider your student's specific needs and your curriculum's objectives. Each tool offers unique features and benefits but comes with its own considerations. Experimentation and adaptation are vital in finding the most effective use of AI in enhancing student learning outcomes.

IMPLEMENTATION GUIDE FOR METHOD 5

Integrating AI into your educational practices can initially seem daunting, but the right approach can significantly enhance your classroom's diversity, inclusivity, and adaptability. By following a structured plan and focusing on the core aspects of your teaching strategy, you can make AI work meaningfully for you and your students. Here's how to do it.

Assess Where AI Should and Shouldn't Be Implemented

Before diving into the world of AI, take a moment to evaluate your current teaching practices and identify areas where AI could make a meaningful impact. Consider repetitive and time-consuming tasks, such as grading quizzes or offering personalized learning paths, as potential candidates for AI intervention. Equally important is recognizing where AI should not replace human interaction—such as fostering emotional support and understanding complex student needs.

Examples to Consider:

- Use AI for personalized learning recommendations but maintain human oversight for sensitive issues like counseling.
- Implement AI tools for administrative tasks to free up more time for direct student interaction.

Start Small

Begin by integrating AI tools that address specific needs rather than overhauling your entire teaching strategy at once. This gradual adaptation to the new technology becomes more accessible for both you and your students.

Steps to Take:

- Choose a single AI tool that can make an immediate impact, such as an AI-powered tutoring system for a particular subject.

- Monitor its effectiveness and student response before scaling up or adding more tools.

Evaluate, Iterate, and Build

Once you've started, continuously assess the impact of AI on your teaching effectiveness and student outcomes. Collect feedback from students to grasp their experience and adjust your methods accordingly. This iterative process ensures that AI integration remains aligned with your educational goals and adapts to the evolving needs of your students.

Key Actions Include:

- Regularly survey students to assess their satisfaction and identify areas for improvement.
- Analyze performance data to see where AI interventions are most effective.

Enhance Learner–Instructor Interaction

Integrating AI into education should augment, not replace, the critical relationship between learners and instructors. Here are detailed guidelines for enhancing this interaction through AI:

Communication Strategies:

- Utilize AI tools to provide immediate feedback on assignments, allowing for more meaningful face-to-face discussions during class time.
- Implement chatbots to answer students' routine

questions, allowing instructors to engage in deeper, more personalized communication.

Support Implementation:

- Leverage AI to monitor student progress and pinpoint those who require additional assistance, guaranteeing they receive support promptly.
- Incorporate AI-driven analytics to tailor support to students' learning styles and needs.

Building a Virtual Presence:

- Create video content or interactive modules where you explain complex topics, using AI to personalize the learning path for each student.
- Use virtual office hours and AI-assisted scheduling to make yourself more available to students for one-on-one consultations.

Practical Guidance with AI:

- Leverage AI to curate and recommend resources that align with each student's learning journey, facilitating a more guided learning experience.
- Employ AI-driven simulations and scenarios in your teaching to provide real-world contexts that enhance understanding and retention.

Fostering Connection:

- Promote AI-facilitated group projects that encourage collaboration and peer learning.
- Use social media and forums integrated with AI to create a community space for students to share experiences and support each other.

Maintaining Diversity, Inclusivity, and Adaptability

In every step of AI integration, ensure that the tools and approaches you choose promote diversity and inclusivity. AI has the potential to offer customized learning experiences that respect and adapt to individual differences—be it in learning styles, speeds, or needs. This personalized approach supports students academically and contributes to a more inclusive environment where every student feels valued and understood.

Considerations for Inclusivity:

- Ensure that AI tools are provided to every student, including those with disabilities, which they can access.
- Pay attention to and address biases within AI algorithms and proactively choose tools that support fairness and diversity.

Integrating AI into your teaching practices offers a promising avenue to enhance the learning experience, making it more personalized, efficient, and inclusive. By starting small, evaluating progress, and enhancing learner-instructor interaction, you can leverage AI to improve academic outcomes and foster a more engaging and supportive classroom environment.

KEY TAKEAWAYS

- Assess where AI can significantly impact your teaching practices, focusing on repetitive tasks and personalized learning while ensuring human oversight remains in sensitive areas.
- Start small by integrating specific AI tools, like AI-powered tutoring systems, to address immediate needs and allow for gradual adjustment.
- Continuously evaluate the effectiveness of AI tools through student feedback and performance data, refining your approach based on these insights.
- Enhance learner–instructor interaction using AI for immediate feedback, chatbots for routine questions, and AI-driven analytics for personalized support.
- Maintain a virtual presence with video content and AI-assisted scheduling to increase availability for one-on-one student consultations.
- Use AI to guide learning with personalized resource recommendations and real-world scenario simulations to enhance understanding.
- Foster social connections through AI-facilitated group projects and community spaces on social media and forums.
- Prioritize diversity, inclusivity, and adaptability by ensuring AI tools are accessible to all students and free from biases.

- Leverage AI to create a flexible and responsive learning environment that adapts to the needs of each student, celebrating the diversity of student abilities and learning styles.
- Stay informed about the latest AI developments to continuously improve and adapt your teaching practices for enhanced learning outcomes.

We've delved into how AI revolutionizes personalized learning, enhancing the experience. You've seen how AI can tailor educational content to meet individual student needs, a testament to technology's role in breaking down barriers to learning. Now, let's pivot to our next venture: Automating Administrative Tasks.

This chapter bridges the gap by showing how the efficiency gained in personalized learning directly translates to the administrative realm. You can reclaim precious time by automating scheduling, grading, and record-keeping tasks, focusing more on what you do best—teaching. Envision a world where you are freed from the burden of paperwork, enabling you to forge deeper connections with your students.

CHAPTER 7
AI-INTEGRATION METHOD 6— AUTOMATING ADMINISTRATIVE TASKS

Picture this: You're juggling a stack of essays to grade, a lesson plan that needs fine-tuning, and an upcoming parent–teacher conference that's been on your mind. The clock ticks loudly, reminding you of the rapidly approaching deadlines. It's a delicate dance, balancing the passion for nurturing young minds with the administrative tasks that pile up seemingly out of nowhere.

You're not alone in this. Teachers everywhere face this tightrope daily, trying to give their best to their students while also managing the behind-the-scenes work that keeps the classroom running smoothly. It's tough, but remember, your effort makes a difference.

NO TIME LEFT FOR TEACHING

Your dedication to your profession is evident as your responsibilities exceed classroom hours. A revealing survey conducted by the EdWeek Research Center, commissioned by the Winston School of Education and Social Policy at

Merrimack College, sheds light on how you allocate your time. The findings show that a typical teacher dedicates 54 hours per week to their profession. Yet, only 46% of this time is spent on direct teaching within the school environment (Hardison, 2022).

Let's delve further into the analysis of these hours. On average, teachers report spending about five hours grading and providing feedback on student work, another five hours planning or preparing lessons, and three hours dealing with general administrative tasks (Hardison, 2022).

Furthermore, you spend three hours engaging in student interactions outside of teaching, two hours collaborating with colleagues, two hours communicating with parents or guardians, and two hours on miscellaneous work tasks. Moreover, tasks such as school committee work, professional development activities, and non-curricular activities like sports or clubs each take up about one hour of your time (Hardison, 2022).

The increasing burden of administrative duties on teachers has sparked concerns regarding the impact on the quality of teaching and learning. It's challenging to stay focused on crafting compelling lesson plans when a big chunk of your time goes toward tasks not directly related to teaching. This shift in focus can inadvertently affect the educational experience for students, as the quality of instruction may suffer due to these additional pressures.

Moreover, balancing non-teaching tasks and fulfilling your core teaching responsibilities is delicate. The dilemma of choosing between sacrificing personal time or student interaction time to complete administrative work is a reality for many. This constant juggling act affects your ability to deliver high-quality education and contributes to teacher burnout, reduced performance, and decreased morale.

With job satisfaction among teachers hitting all-time lows, partly due to the intensified schedules since the pandemic, it's crucial to address how these additional responsibilities impact your well-being and professional satisfaction.

The relationship between non-teaching tasks and teacher burnout is complex. Burnout not only affects your health and well-being but also influences your performance in the classroom, which can lead to a decrease in student engagement and achievement. Maintaining a high level of morale is essential for fostering a positive learning environment; however, the added stress from administrative duties can make this increasingly difficult.

FOCUS ON TEACHING; AI WILL TAKE CARE OF THE REST

AI is transforming how educators handle administrative duties, enabling them to prioritize teaching as their primary focus.

By integrating AI-powered tools, schools can significantly reduce the time teachers spend on administrative duties, thus enabling them to dedicate more energy and attention to guiding and instructing students. This transformation is not just about adopting new technologies; it's about strategically enhancing the efficiency and effectiveness of educational processes.

You often find yourself overwhelmed by administrative tasks, from grading assignments to managing attendance and compiling reports. A study by EdChoice highlights that teachers spend a considerable portion of their time on non-instructional activities, which reduces their availability for student interaction and instructional preparation (McCarroll, 2022).

The burden of these tasks contributes to educator burnout, with many considering leaving the profession earlier than planned, exacerbated by the pandemic's impact on staffing and workload.

AI comes to the rescue in several areas, particularly grading, where it can efficiently evaluate multiple-choice and fill-in-the-blank tests. Developers are creating increasingly sophisticated AI systems that evaluate open-ended questions, showcasing AI's expanding capability to manage various grading responsibilities.

Attendance management is another area where AI excels. It can accurately track attendance, generate insightful reports on student attendance trends, and help identify issues like chronic absenteeism, which affects a significant portion of students nationwide.

AI facilitates more effective communication through chatbots and virtual assistants, which can handle routine inquiries and scheduling tasks, freeing you up for more meaningful student interactions. This adoption of AI chatbots by educational institutions is becoming increasingly common, offering a glimpse into the future of educational administrative efficiency.

AI-powered tools help you cut down on administrative tasks, freeing you up to focus on your core strength: teaching. This shift not only enhances the educational experience for students but also addresses the issue of educator burnout by alleviating some of the most time-consuming tasks.

COMMON ADMINISTRATIVE TASKS AND HOW TO AUTOMATE THEM WITH AI

In the dynamic world of education, managing events and extracurricular activities can be quite a handful for teachers. Many AI tools are now available to significantly lighten this load, automating tasks from scheduling to budgeting and documentation. Let's dive into some tools that can transform how you organize and manage school events and activities.

Managing Events and Extracurricular Activities

ChatGPT

- **Overview and features:** ChatGPT, developed by OpenAI, is a versatile AI chatbot that can assist in drafting emails, planning events, and generating creative content for documentation. It's beneficial for brainstorming ideas for events, creating plan outlines, and drafting necessary communications.
- **How it helps:**

  ○ **Scheduling the event:** Generate ideas and create detailed event plans.
  ○ **Preparing documentation:** Draft emails, invitations, and informational materials.

- **Access and pricing:** ChatGPT is accessible via OpenAI's website, with various pricing tiers, including a free version with limited capabilities and a subscription model for more advanced features.
- **Examples:** Use ChatGPT to draft a sports day welcome speech or create a checklist for your next field trip.
- **Pros and cons:** ChatGPT is highly versatile and easy to use, but it may require manual adjustments and fact-checking for accuracy.

Taskade

- **Overview and features:** Taskade facilitates team organization, project management, and real-time collaboration, aiming to assist teams in coordinating tasks effectively. It's perfect for coordinating the many moving parts of school events and extracurricular activities.
- **How it helps:**

  ○ **Organizing extracurricular activities:** Create shared project spaces for each event.
  ○ **Allocating resources:** Assign tasks and responsibilities to staff and volunteers.
  ○ **Scheduling the event:** Use the integrated calendar and task lists.

- **Access and pricing:** Available at taskade.com, Taskade offers a free version with essential features and paid plans for additional capabilities.

- **Examples:** Use Taskade to create a shared workspace for the annual science fair, with tasks and deadlines for each part of the event.
- **Pros and cons:** Great for collaboration and organization, but might be overwhelming for smaller, more spartan events due to its extensive features.

Notion

- **Overview and features:** Notion acts as a comprehensive workspace enabling writing, planning, collaboration, and organization in one platform. It's perfect for creating centralized documentation and planning resources for events.
- **How it helps:**

  - **Creating a budget:** Use templates to track expenses and budget allocations.
  - **Preparing documentation:** Store all event-related documents in one place.

- **Access and Pricing:** Notion is accessible via Notion.com with a free plan for individuals and pricing tiers for teams and organizations.
- **Examples:** Create a comprehensive event planning document in Notion, including schedules, budgets, and resource lists.
- **Pros and cons:** Notion is incredibly flexible and customizable, but its wide range of features can be daunting for new users.

Gatherly

- **Overview and features:** Gatherly is a platform for hosting virtual and hybrid events. It's ideal for organizing online extracurricular activities, seminars, and meetings, providing a space for interactive and engaging virtual gatherings.
- **How it helps:**

  ○ **Scheduling the event:** Easy setup for virtual events.
  ○ **Allocating resources:** Plan and manage virtual space for different activities.

- **Access and pricing:** You can find information about Gatherly's products and pricing on their website, usually determined by the size and duration of your event.
- **Examples:** Host a virtual open day for parents and students, with different 'rooms' for various presentations and Q and A sessions.
- **Pros and cons:** Gatherly offers an engaging platform for virtual events but may require a learning curve for those unfamiliar with hosting online gatherings.

Splash

- **Overview and features:** Splash is an event marketing platform that helps you create event pages, send invitations, and track RSVPs. It's handy for managing school events' guest lists and promotional aspects.

- **How it helps:**

  ○ **Scheduling the event:** Create beautiful event pages with all the necessary details.
  ○ **Creating a budget:** Track sign-ups and manage event resources accordingly.

- **Access and pricing:** Splash provides various pricing levels, including a free tier for basic event planning needs. Visit their website for more details.
- **Examples:** Use Splash to create an attractive landing page for your next seminar, complete with registration forms and event information.
- **Pros and cons:** Splash excels in event promotion and design but focuses less on in-depth planning and budgeting aspects of event management.

Leveraging these AI tools can significantly streamline the planning and execution of school events and extracurricular activities, allowing you to focus more on delivering enriching student experiences.

Printing or Photocopying Class Learning Resources

In the dynamic world of education, teachers constantly seek innovative tools to streamline their administrative tasks, particularly in preparing and managing learning resources. Let's dive into a curated list of AI tools that are game-changers in this domain, discussing their features, accessibility, pricing, and practical applications.

Jasper Art

- **Overview and features:** Jasper Art is an AI-driven platform that excels in creating visually appealing educational materials. It can automatically adjust fonts, layouts, and styles, making your documents engaging and readable.
- **How it helps:** Automatically formats learning resources, ensuring they are captivating and accessible for all students.
- **Access and pricing:** Available online, Jasper Art offers tiered pricing plans to fit different needs, including specific options for educators.
- **Usage guide:** Input your content and specify your desired aesthetic (e.g., "friendly and engaging for middle school students"), and Jasper Art will do the rest, generating ready-to-print materials.
- **Pros and cons:** While Jasper Art dramatically enhances the visual appeal of educational materials, its reliance on AI for design choices might not always align with specific academic standards or preferences.

TinyWow

- **Overview and features:** TinyWow is a multipurpose tool that simplifies document conversion, compression, and preparation for printing.
- **How it helps:** It can optimize files for printing, reducing the load on printing queues by compressing files without losing quality.

- **Access and pricing:** Free to use via its website, making it an excellent option for you on a budget.
- **Usage guide:** Upload your educational materials to TinyWow, select the desired optimization, and download the print-ready files in moments.
- **Pros and cons:** TinyWow offers a high level of user-friendliness at no cost, though its capabilities may be less extensive when compared to dedicated formatting tools.

Evernote

- **Overview and features:** Evernote is a note-taking and organization tool ideal for managing and sharing educational resources.
- **How it helps:** Teachers can create, format, and organize learning materials efficiently, sharing them directly with students or for printing.
- **Access and pricing:** Evernote offers free and premium plans, accessible online and through its app.
- **Usage guide:** Organize your teaching materials into notebooks, use templates for consistent formatting, and share links with students or the print queue.
- **Pros and cons:** Evernote's versatility in organizing and sharing materials is unmatched, though the advanced features require a subscription.

EtherPad

- **Overview and features:** EtherPad provides a collaborative writing platform perfect for real-time document editing and formatting.
- **How it helps:** Facilitates the collaborative creation and automatic formatting of educational materials.
- **Access and pricing:** Open-source and free, EtherPad is accessible via its website.
- **Usage guide:** Let's set up a collaborative workspace, invite students or co-teachers, and collaborate on preparing materials easily formatted for printing.
- **Pros and cons:** Its real-time collaboration feature is a significant plus, but EtherPad lacks advanced formatting tools.

Bit.ai

- **Overview and features:** www.Bit.ai is a document collaboration platform for interactive and multimedia educational materials.
- **How it helps:** Automatically formats documents and integrates various media types, making resources more engaging.
- **Access and pricing:** Offers tiered pricing plans, including discounts, accessible online.
- **Usage guide:** Create a document, use the intuitive editor to add text, images, and videos, and export or print directly from the platform.
- **Pros and cons:** Bit.ai is excellent for creating multimedia resources, but the cost might be prohibitive.

LogicalDoc

- **Overview and features:** LogicalDoc is an advanced document management system that offers features to automate the organization and prioritization of printing tasks.
- **How it helps:** Optimizes printing queues based on urgency, priority, or resource constraints, significantly reducing the manual effort in managing print jobs.
- **Access and pricing:** It comes with various pricing plans, including options suitable for educational institutions, accessible through its website.
- **Usage guide:** Upload documents, set priorities, and let LogicalDoc manage the printing queue efficiently.
- **Pros and cons:** LogicalDoc excels in document management and queue optimization but might require a learning curve to utilize its features thoroughly.

By integrating these AI tools into your teaching routine, you can cut down significantly on the time dedicated to administrative duties, enabling you to prioritize teaching over paperwork. By selecting the right tools that fit your specific needs and budget, you can streamline your workload and potentially transform the learning experience for your students.

Collating Student Records and Performance Reports

Leveraging AI tools for collating student records and performance reports can significantly enhance the efficiency and accuracy of administrative reporting. Here's a curated list of AI tools tailored for you to streamline the process of generating detailed reports on student performance, behavior, and other crucial metrics.

ReportCardComments

- **Overview and features:** ReportCardComments aims to simplify the task of crafting comprehensive student report comments, reducing the workload associated with this aspect of report writing. It provides tailored templates and recommendations to showcase every student's accomplishments and areas needing development.
- **Addressing efficiency and accuracy:** By automating the comment generation process, this tool ensures consistency and reduces errors in student reports.
- **Access and pricing:** Available online, with free and premium subscription options to suit different needs.
- **Usage guide:** Enter student performance data. The tool suggests relevant comments, which you can then personalize. An example might be inputting a student's grades and areas of interest to generate a personalized comment.
- **Pros and cons:** The significant advantages are time-saving and customization. However, the comments might need more personalization if not reviewed.

ReportCards.ai

- **Overview and features:** This AI tool transforms raw student data into comprehensive report cards, incorporating academic performance, behavior, and extracurricular activities.
- **Addressing efficiency and accuracy:** It simplifies creating report cards, guaranteeing precise and thorough reports with minimal work.
- **Access and pricing:** You can access it online, with pricing tailored to your institution's size and requirements.
- **Usage guide:** Input student data and let AI generate a full report card. For instance, entering a student's grades, attendance, and teacher comments could produce a detailed report card.
- **Pros and cons:** It's highly efficient and customizable but may require manual checks to capture student performance nuances accurately.

MagicSchool.ai

- **Overview and features:** www.MagicSchool.ai offers a broader administrative solution, including performance reporting, attendance tracking, and more, using AI to simplify complex data.
- **Addressing efficiency and accuracy:** This tool helps report, manage, and analyze student data comprehensively.
- **Access and pricing:** It's a web-based service with tiered pricing to accommodate different school sizes.

- **Usage guide:** After setting up your school's profile, you can start inputting data across different metrics for the AI to analyze and report. An example might be analyzing trends in student attendance and correlating them with academic performance.
- **Pros and cons:** Offers a wide range of features but might be overwhelming for smaller schools with limited needs.

Education Copilot

- **Overview and features:** This tool assists in crafting and monitoring performance metrics customized to suit the specific needs of each student for their individualized learning plans.
- **Addressing efficiency and accuracy:** It facilitates personalized education strategies by tracking progress and suggesting adjustments.
- **Access and pricing:** Available online, with various subscription models based on the number of students and the depth of features required.
- **Usage guide:** Enter student-specific goals and performance data to receive personalized reports and suggestions. Examples of goals are tracking a student's progress in math and recommending focused activities.
- **Pros and cons:** Great for personalized learning plans but may require significant initial setup time.

These AI tools can dramatically improve how you manage student data and performance reporting. Selecting the appropriate tool tailored to your requirements enables you to save time, minimize mistakes, and prioritize delivering top-notch education.

Parent–Teacher Communications

In the digital age, efficient parent–teacher communication is pivotal for students' educational success. Let's dive into some recommended AI tools that can transform your communication strategies, making them more effective and less time-consuming.

Wordtune

- **Overview and features:** Wordtune is an AI-powered writing assistant that helps you craft clear and more engaging messages. It's handy for composing newsletters, announcements, and personalized messages to parents.
- **Addressing communication needs:** It streamlines the communication process by suggesting improvements to your writing, making your messages more understandable and engaging for parents.
- **Access and pricing:** With free and paid plan options, you can access it as a browser extension or on wordtune.com.
- **Guide and examples:** Write your draft message, and use Wordtune to refine it. An example is turning a complex sentence into something more digestible for busy parents.
- **Prompt tips:** Use it to rephrase sentences for clarity and impact.

- **Pros and cons:** Great for enhancing message clarity, but relies on your initial draft.

TalkingPoints

- **Overview and features:** An education technology platform that breaks down language barriers between teachers and parents, enabling text message communication in multiple languages.
- **Addressing communication needs:** Facilitates seamless, inclusive communication with all parents, regardless of language differences.
- **Access and pricing:** Via their website and mobile app. Free and premium plans are available.
- **Guide and examples:** Teachers can send a message in English automatically translated into the parent's preferred language.
- **Prompt tips:** Use simple sentences to ensure accurate translation.
- **Pros and cons:** Highly inclusive, though translation accuracy can vary.

MagicSchool AI

- **Overview and features:** Currently conceptual, MagicSchool AI aims to personalize communication by analyzing parent engagement and preferences.
- **Addressing communication needs:** Could tailor communications based on parental engagement, making messages more relevant.
- **Access and pricing:** Access the platform through its

website. Available in free and subscription-based pricing.

- **Guide and examples:** Potentially, it would automate sending personalized updates based on parent interaction history.
- **Pros and cons:** Highly personalized communication potential, but privacy concerns and implementation specifics remain unclear.

ChatGPT

- **Overview and features:** An AI model capable of generating human-like text based on prompts, helpful for drafting diverse types of communications.
- **Addressing communication needs:** Can help compose newsletters and announcements and provide prompt communication tips.
- **Access and pricing:** The OpenAI platform offers free and paid tier options and integrations with various services.
- **Guide and examples:** Input a brief outline of your message, and let ChatGPT draft it. An example is creating engaging announcements.
- **Prompt tips:** Be specific with your prompts to generate more targeted content.
- **Pros and cons:** Highly versatile, though outcomes may require fine-tuning for personal touch.

Klassly

- **Overview and features:** This classroom communication app fosters collaboration among teachers, parents, and students.
- **Addressing communication needs:** Enables sharing of announcements and homework assignments and facilitates direct messaging.
- **Access and pricing:** Available on web and mobile platforms. Free with optional premium features.
- **Guide and examples:** Teachers can post classroom updates and homework, which parents receive instantly.
- **Prompt tips:** Regularly update your class space with engaging content and visuals.
- **Pros and cons:** Encourages active community but might require consistent engagement to be effective.

ParentSquare

- **Overview and features:** A comprehensive platform for school-home communication that integrates with school systems for a unified experience.
- **Addressing communication needs:** Offers newsletters, direct messaging, and event organization in one platform.
- **Access and pricing:** Web and mobile app. Custom pricing based on school needs.
- **Guide and examples:** Easily distribute a school-wide newsletter or a personalized message to specific parents.

- **Prompt tips:** Utilize the analytics feature to track engagement and tailor your communication strategy accordingly.
- **Pros and cons:** Comprehensive features, but might be overwhelming for new users.

Remind

- **Overview and features:** A messaging app designed for education allows safe and simple communication between you and your student's parents.
- **Addressing communication needs:** Simplifies sending reminders, assignments, and scheduling parent–teacher conferences.
- **Access and pricing:** Web, iOS, and Android apps. Free basic service, with a premium tier for additional features.
- **Guide and examples:** Set up class codes, and parents can subscribe to receive updates and reminders directly to their phones.
- **Prompt tips:** Plan to send messages in advance for consistent communication.
- **Pros and cons:** Easy to use, but with limited functionality.

ClassTag

- **Overview and features:** A platform that transforms how you connect with parents through messaging, conferences, and volunteer organization.
- **Addressing communication needs:** Streamlines

communication and engagement with parents through various tools.

- **Access and pricing:** Available on the web and through mobile apps. Free for teachers, with optional premium services.
- **Guide and examples:** Teachers can send weekly newsletters and automate parent–teacher conference scheduling.
- **Prompt tips:** Encourage parent engagement by utilizing ClassTag's rewards system.
- **Pros and cons:** Offers robust features for engagement but may require time to navigate the comprehensive platform.

Each tool has unique strengths and potential drawbacks, but collectively, they offer a suite of options to revolutionize how you communicate with parents. By leveraging these AI-driven tools, you can ensure your messages are clear, engaging, and accessible to all parents, fostering a stronger school community and supporting student success.

Attendance Monitoring

In today's digital era, where efficiency and automation are at the forefront of educational administration, AI tools for attendance monitoring are becoming increasingly indispensable. Let's explore some suggested tools to revolutionize attendance monitoring in academic environments.

ClickUp

- **Overview and features:** ClickUp is a versatile project management tool with time-tracking features, allowing for automated attendance tracking. Its functionalities encompass assigning tasks, setting reminders, and monitoring the time dedicated to particular tasks or activities.
- **Addressing attendance monitoring:** Using the Time Tracking ClickApp within ClickUp, you can monitor attendance and participation in tasks or projects, providing a clear overview of student engagement.
- **Access and pricing:** ClickUp can be accessed at ClickUp's website and is available on desktop and mobile platforms. Offers a free version with basic features; paid plans provide more advanced options and greater flexibility in tracking and reporting.
- **URL:** clickup.com
- **How to use it:** To use ClickUp for attendance, first enable the Time Tracking ClickApp for your space. Then, track attendance by starting a timer for each student engaging in classroom activities or projects.
- **Pros and cons:** Pros include its versatility and integrative capacity with other tools. Cons might be the learning curve for those unfamiliar with project management software.

Clockify

- **Overview and features:** Clockify, an app for tracking time and creating timesheets, enables you to monitor hours spent on different projects. It's ideal for attendance monitoring because it offers detailed insights into time consumption.

- **Addressing attendance monitoring:** Clockify can track student attendance by logging students' time on educational activities or in class.
- **Access and pricing:** Available at Clockify's website and mobile apps. Free for basic use, with premium features available for a fee.
- **URL:** clockify.me
- **How to use it:** Set up projects or classes in Clockify and have students start and stop the timer as they attend sessions or work on assignments, providing an automated way to monitor attendance.
- **Pros and cons:** One advantage is its user-friendly interface and complimentary access to fundamental functionalities, while a drawback could be students having to initiate and terminate it manually.

Time Doctor

- **Overview and features:** Time Doctor is a time tracking and productivity monitoring tool designed to help manage remote teams but can be adapted for educational purposes to track attendance and student engagement.
- **Addressing attendance monitoring:** It provides tracking time, captures screenshots, and generates comprehensive reports, enabling educators to verify students' attendance and engagement in online classes or homework activities.
- **Access and pricing:** Find it at Time Doctor's

website. It is a paid service with various plans based on the number of users and required features.

- **URL:** www.timedoctor.com
- **How to use it:** You can create tasks or classes in Time Doctor and monitor the time students log in real-time or through reports, making attendance tracking straightforward and automated.
- **Pros and cons:** The software's comprehensive tracking features constitute a significant advantage, while its cost and potential privacy concerns might be drawbacks for some educational settings.

Everhour

- **Overview and features:** Everhour integrates directly with many project management tools, offering seamless time tracking and reporting functionalities.
- **Addressing attendance monitoring:** By embedding directly into supported project management platforms, Everhour can track students' time on assignments or projects, facilitating attendance monitoring.
- **Access and Pricing:** Accessible at Everhour's website. The service provides a free trial period and then transitions to a subscription-based model.
- **URL:** everhour.com
- **How to use it:** Integrate Everhour with your project management tool, then use it to track each student's time on tasks or activities associated with their attendance.
- **Pros and cons:** Its seamless integration with other tools is a pro; however, dependence on third-party

project management software might be considered a con.

Whether through direct time tracking, integration with project management tools, or detailed productivity monitoring, these AI solutions offer varied approaches to suit different educational needs and settings. The key is to select the tool that best aligns with your specific requirements, ensuring an efficient and effective attendance monitoring process.

IMPLEMENTATION GUIDE FOR METHOD 6

Integrating AI tools into your educational practices can significantly reduce the burden of non-teaching tasks, allowing you to focus more on what truly matters: educating and inspiring your students. Here's how you can smoothly transition into using AI to automate administrative tasks, ensuring you leverage technology most effectively and sensitively.

Assess Where AI Should and Shouldn't Be Implemented

First off, take a moment to evaluate your daily tasks and identify areas where AI could be most beneficial. Recognizing that only some tasks are appropriate for AI automation is crucial. For instance, AI can streamline grading multiple-choice tests or managing class schedules, but it may not be the best at handling sensitive student interactions or creating nuanced lesson plans. The goal here is to find a balance where AI handles the repetitive, time-consuming tasks, freeing you up to engage more personally and creatively with your students.

Start Small

Diving headfirst into AI might seem tempting, but starting with small, manageable changes is wise. Introduce an AI tool to tackle a specific task, such as tracking attendance or organizing student feedback. This approach lets you get comfortable with the technology and understand its impact on your workflow without overwhelming yourself or your students. Small wins will build your confidence and demonstrate the tangible benefits of AI, making the transition smoother for everyone involved.

Evaluate, Iterate, and Build

Incorporating AI involves more than a single action. It requires ongoing engagement and adaptation. It's a cycle of evaluation, iteration, and building. After integrating an AI tool, take time to assess its effectiveness. Is it saving you time? How is it affecting student engagement? Gathering your own experiences and your students' feedback is invaluable. Use this information to tweak how you use AI tools or decide if a different tool might better meet your needs. This ongoing process ensures that your AI tools remain aligned with your educational goals and adapt to changing needs.

Collaborate and Communicate

As you embark on this journey, remember that your colleagues are valuable allies. You can gain insights and support to integrate AI into your teaching practices effectively by collaborating and communicating with them. Share your experiences, challenges, and successes. Different educators have experimented with other tools or strategies that could be beneficial. Furthermore, openly discussing with students the purpose and implementation of AI in their education can ease worries and cultivate a culture of trust and creativity.

By following these guidelines, you can harness the power of AI to reduce the burden of administrative tasks, allowing you to dedicate more time and energy to the core of your profession: teaching and inspiring your students.

KEY TAKEAWAYS

- Administrative duties can detract from teaching quality and contribute to burnout.
- AI technology can alleviate administrative burdens, allowing teachers to focus more on teaching.
- AI aids in grading, attendance management, and communication tasks.
- Adopting AI in education reduces the administrative workload and addresses teacher burnout.
- AI tools can streamline event management by assisting in scheduling, resource allocation, documentation, and virtual event hosting.

- AI tools aid in preparing and formatting learning resources for printing or photocopying, offering features like automatic formatting, document conversion, organization, and queue optimization.
- AI tools automate the process of collating student records and generating performance reports, enhancing efficiency and accuracy in administrative reporting.
- AI tools revolutionize parent–teacher communication through AI-powered writing assistance, language translation, personalized messaging, and comprehensive communication platforms.
- AI tools transform attendance monitoring with features like time tracking, project integration, productivity monitoring, and detailed reporting, catering to various educational needs and settings.

In this chapter, you've explored how AI can lighten your administrative load, giving you more time to focus on what truly matters: teaching. From grading to communication, AI offers solutions to everyday challenges, addressing burnout and improving efficiency. Now, let's delve into turning AI challenges into opportunities for educational growth.

CHAPTER 8

TURNING AI CHALLENGES INTO OPPORTUNITIES FOR EDUCATIONAL GROWTH

Integrating AI into education marks the beginning of an innovative era, but it also brings challenges. Tackling these challenges head-on means embracing a mindset shift toward adaptability and lifelong learning within educational realms. This evolution requires recognizing AI's potential to revolutionize interactions between you and your students, enhance personalized learning, and improve feedback mechanisms.

However, it's essential to navigate the pitfalls, such as algorithmic bias, with a strategic approach emphasizing human-centered AI, aligning with educational goals, and upholding trust and safety for all involved.

CHALLENGE 1: DATA PROTECTION AND STUDENT PRIVACY

Protecting sensitive information is crucial in an era where digital footprints expand with every click. Schools and educational institutions are treasure troves of personal data ranging from students' academic records to their details. The challenge is to protect this information from unauthorized access and to create an environment where students and parents are confident in the security measures.

Opportunity: Cultivating a Culture of Privacy and Security

This challenge, however, opens the door to an invaluable opportunity: the chance to cultivate a culture of privacy and security. Your unique position enables you to set an example by highlighting the significance of data protection with thorough digital literacy programs. By integrating privacy education into the curriculum, you not only arm students with the knowledge to protect their data but also instill a lifelong respect for privacy.

Implementing Robust Security Measures

Begin with the basics: Ensure that all digital tools and platforms comply with local and international data protection regulations, such as the General Data Protection Regulation (GDPR) or the Children's Online Privacy Protection Act (COPPA). Regular audits and updates of security protocols can fortify defenses against cyber threats.

Empowering Students and Parents

Empowerment comes through education. Workshops for students and information sessions for parents can demystify data protection, highlighting practical steps for safeguarding personal information online. Encourage students to adopt safe online practices by crafting solid and unique passwords and carefully considering the information they share on social media platforms.

Leveraging Technology for Privacy

Technological solutions can be allies in the quest for data protection. Employ privacy-enhancing technologies (PETs) to reduce the risk of data breaches and secure data collection, storage, and processing. Encourage the adoption of encrypted communication tools and secure file-sharing services to protect the integrity of student data.

Fostering Open Dialogue

Establish an environment that proactively addresses privacy concerns instead of just acknowledging them. Encourage students, parents, and staff to voice their questions and concerns regarding data protection, fostering a transparent dialogue about the measures to secure their information.

Building Partnerships

Collaborate with cybersecurity experts, legal professionals, and privacy advocates to stay abreast of the latest trends and threats in data protection. These partnerships can provide valuable insights and resources for enhancing your institution's privacy posture.

Case Studies and Real-World Examples

Include real-world examples and case studies of data breaches and privacy issues in the curriculum. Discussing the consequences of such incidents highlights the importance of vigilance and brings abstract concepts to life, making the lessons more relatable and impactful.

Continuous Learning and Improvement

Keep your knowledge and skills in data protection up to date, adapting your strategies to tackle new threats as the digital landscape evolves. Encourage a culture of continuous learning among your colleagues and students, reinforcing the idea that data protection is a shared responsibility.

While daunting, the challenge of data protection and student privacy is manageable. By transforming this challenge into an opportunity for education, empowerment, and engagement, you can pave the way for a safer digital future. Embrace the role of a privacy advocate, educating and inspiring your students to navigate the digital world with confidence and caution. Together, you can build a foundation of trust and security that extends beyond the classroom, preparing students for academic success and responsible citizenship in the digital age.

CHALLENGE 2: EQUAL ACCESS TO TECHNOLOGY

In many communities, students face unequal opportunities to access technology. The reasons range from economic disparities, which prevent families from affording personal computers or high-speed internet to geographic challenges, where rural or remote areas need more infrastructure for reliable internet connectivity. Additionally, schools in underfunded districts often need help to provide up-to-date technology for their students, further widening the gap.

The digital divide significantly impacts the fairness of educational opportunities. Students need reliable access to technology at home to complete digital assignments, participate in online learning, and acquire digital literacy skills critical for success in the 21st century. Moreover, the shift to online learning, accelerated by the COVID-19 pandemic, has highlighted and exacerbated these disparities, revealing a stark contrast in educational access and outcomes based on students' technological resources.

Opportunity: Bridging the Digital Divide Through Innovative Solutions

While daunting, the challenge of equal access to technology presents an opportunity for educators, policymakers, and communities to come together and forge innovative solutions to bridge the digital divide. Here are strategies to transform this challenge into an opportunity for better learning and growth:

Community and Public–Private Partnerships

Partnering with local businesses, non-profits, and technology companies can offer resources to support schools and students in need. These partnerships can result in hardware donations, funding for technology upgrades, and the development of community internet access points, such as public Wi-Fi zones in libraries and community centers.

Grants and Funding for Technology Access

You can seek grants and funding opportunities to improve school technology access. Federal and state programs and private foundations often offer financial support for purchasing devices, upgrading internet infrastructure, or implementing technology-driven educational programs.

Adopting Flexible Learning Models

Schools can adopt more flexible learning models to accommodate students with limited access to technology. This might include hybrid approaches that blend online and offline learning activities, ensuring that students without home internet can still engage with the curriculum. Ensuring all students have equal learning opportunities requires providing physical materials for home use and digital activities for in-school use.

Technology Lending Programs

Schools can develop technology lending programs allowing students to check out home-use devices. This approach ensures that students can access the technology they need to complete assignments and participate in digital learning, regardless of their economic status.

Digital Literacy Training for All

Equal access to technology also means ensuring that students, teachers, and parents have the necessary skills to use technology effectively. Schools can offer digital literacy workshops and training sessions, empowering the entire school community to navigate the digital world confidently.

Advocating for Policy Change

You and community members can advocate for local, state, and federal policy changes to prioritize funding and support for technology access in education. This can include lobbying for expanding broadband infrastructure in underserved areas and policies that provide schools with the financial resources needed to update and maintain technology.

Transforming Challenge Into Opportunity

By addressing the challenge of equal access to technology head-on, you can bridge the digital divide and create more inclusive, equitable learning environments. These efforts guarantee that every student has the tools to thrive in a digital world, regardless of background.

The journey toward equal technology access is a collaborative effort requiring the commitment of educators, policymakers, and the community. It's about more than just handing out devices. It's about creating an equal playing field to ensure every student can succeed in the digital era. By turning this challenge into an opportunity, we can foster a culture of innovation, resilience, and inclusivity that prepares all students for the future.

CHALLENGE 3: RELIABILITY OF INFORMATION

In today's information age, the internet is a vast ocean of data, with waves of information accessible at our fingertips. However, not all info floating in this digital sea is reliable or accurate. The challenge here lies in discerning the quality of information, which is paramount for you and your students. The quality and quantity of information significantly influence its value. High-quality data is accurate, unbiased, and comprehensive, providing a solid foundation for knowledge and learning. Conversely, poor-quality information can mislead, misinform, and, at worst, propagate falsehoods.

The challenge increases as the available information becomes overwhelmingly vast. While having abundant resources can be seen as advantageous, verifying the reliability and accuracy of information is more daunting. You often grapple with ensuring that the content you provide or endorse is engaging and informative but also accurate and trustworthy.

Opportunity: Cultivating Critical Thinkers

Transforming this challenge into an opportunity begins with a shift in perspective. Rather than viewing the reliability of information solely as a hurdle, you can use it as a springboard for teaching critical thinking and research skills. Here's how:

Promote Information Literacy

Show students how to assess the reliability of sources. Encourage them to look for information from reputable sources, check author credentials and publication dates, and cross-reference facts across multiple sources. By instilling these habits, you can turn the challenge of information reliability into an opportunity to develop savvy, discerning information consumers.

Foster a Questioning Mindset

Motivate students to critically evaluate the information they encounter. This pertains not only to external sources but also to classroom content. By fostering a culture where questioning is welcomed and pursued, you cultivate critical thinkers who are less likely to accept information at face value.

Engage in Real-World Problem Solving

Use current events or real-world problems as a basis for assignments. Assign students the task of exploring these topics through diverse sources. This not only aids in understanding the issue at hand but also allows students to practice discerning the reliability of different types of information.

Incorporate Collaborative Learning

Group projects can be a dynamic way for students to engage with various sources of information. Through collaboration, students can share the responsibility of vetting information and learning from one another about the criteria for evaluating data reliability.

Utilize Technology and Tool

Leverage digital tools that assist in evaluating the credibility of sources. Various online platforms and libraries offer resources specifically designed to help users discern the quality of information. Educating students on these tools can empower them to independently assess the reliability of data.

Reflect and Discuss

Regular discussions about the information encountered in and outside the classroom can reinforce the importance of reliability. Sharing experiences of encountering misinformation can be particularly enlightening, offering teachable moments for you and your students.

By addressing the challenge of information reliability through these approaches, you can transform a potential obstacle into a valuable learning opportunity. This improves students' learning experiences and equips them with the confidence and critical understanding needed to confidently navigate today's complex information landscape.

CHALLENGE 4: PLAGIARISM AND CHEATING

Plagiarism and cheating stem from various factors, including pressure to succeed, lack of understanding about plagiarism, and, sometimes, a perceived lack of consequences. In the digital era, students often find the boundaries between research and plagiarism fading due to the ease of accessing information. Conversely, cheating often comes from the pressure to meet high academic standards and the fear of failure. These behaviors undermine the educational process and impede personal and intellectual growth.

Research indicates a significant prevalence of these issues in academic settings. A study by McCabe, Trevino, and Butterfield found that over 60% of college students admit to some form of cheating during their academic careers (*Facts and Statistics*, n.d.). This statistic underscores the problem's extensive reach and emphasizes the necessity of developing effective strategies to tackle it.

Opportunity: Fostering Integrity and Skills Development

The challenge of plagiarism and cheating presents an opportunity for you to foster an environment of integrity while emphasizing the development of critical skills.

Educating on Ethics and Integrity

Begin by establishing a clear and comprehensive policy on academic honesty. Educate students about what constitutes plagiarism and cheating, emphasizing the importance of ethics and integrity in both academic and professional settings. Workshops, seminars, and orientation sessions can effectively convey these principles.

Developing Critical Thinking and Research Skills

Many instances of plagiarism arise from a need for more understanding of adequately citing sources or synthesizing information. Incorporating lessons on research methodologies, citation practices, and how to engage with and interpret sources critically can empower students to produce original work confidently.

Creating a Culture of Accountability

Foster a learning environment where students take responsibility for their and their peers' learning. Peer review exercises and honor codes can cultivate a sense of responsibility and community, discouraging dishonest practices.

Utilizing Technology Wisely

Leverage technology to both prevent and educate. Use plagiarism detection software as a deterrent and a teaching tool, helping students understand how to avoid plagiarism. Moreover, integrating technology responsibly in coursework can make cheating more complex and less appealing.

Encouraging Open Communication

Foster an environment that encourages students to discuss their academic challenges openly. Open lines of communication can help students feel more supported and less likely to resort to dishonest measures.

Promoting Growth Mindset

Encourage a growth mindset, focusing on learning and development rather than simply on grades. This approach helps students to see challenges as opportunities for growth, reducing the temptation to engage in academic dishonesty.

Individualizing Assessments

Tailor assessments to reduce opportunities for cheating. Personalized questions or projects, oral exams, and in-class evaluations can make it more challenging for students to engage in dishonest behavior.

Implementing Solutions: Practical Steps

Taking practical steps to implement these opportunities can significantly mitigate the challenges of plagiarism and cheating:

- **Clear guidelines:** Clearly articulate the expectations and consequences related to academic dishonesty at the start of each course.
- **Resources and support:** Provide students with resources on citation styles and access to workshops or tutoring on academic writing and ethics.

- **Assessment variety:** Use various assessment methods to cater to different learning styles and reduce the feasibility of cheating.
- **Feedback and revision:** Allow students to submit drafts for feedback before the final submission to encourage learning and improvement.
- **Academic integrity pledge:** Incorporate an integrity pledge that students sign at the course's beginning, reinforcing the issue's seriousness.

The Way Forward

Transforming the challenge of plagiarism and cheating into an opportunity for growth requires a multifaceted approach that involves educating, engaging, and empowering students. By fostering a culture of integrity and accountability, you can address these challenges and equip students with the skills and ethical foundation necessary for success beyond the classroom.

CHALLENGE 5: ALGORITHM BIAS

When humans create computer systems, the systems often mirror the creators' implicit values, including their prejudices and assumptions, leading to algorithm bias. This can manifest in various ways, from search engines that perpetuate stereotypes to predictive policing systems that disproportionately target minority communities. Algorithm bias is not just a technical issue but a teachable moment about ethics, fairness, and the importance of diversity in technology.

The Nature of the Bias

Algorithms, by themselves, are neutral mathematical formulas. Their creators' data input and design decisions can introduce biases into them. For example, if a facial recognition system is trained primarily on images of light-skinned individuals, it will be less accurate in identifying individuals with darker skin tones. This has real-world implications, from misidentification in legal contexts to unequal user experiences in consumer technology.

Bias can also stem from the objectives set by those deploying the algorithm. Suppose an online job platform optimizes search results for "ideal" candidates based on historical hiring data. In that case, it may inadvertently favor candidates from certain demographic groups over others, perpetuating existing inequalities.

Impact on Education

Algorithm bias in the educational context can influence various areas, from standardized testing tools to educational software. This bias affects identifying students for special education services, advanced programs, or disciplinary actions. Recognizing and addressing these biases is crucial for creating an equitable learning environment.

Opportunity: Fostering Critical Thinking and Inclusivity in Tech

Empowering Critical Thinkers

One of the most potent opportunities arising from the challenge of algorithm bias is the chance to teach students critical thinking skills. Encouraging students to question the technology they use, its underlying data, and the context of its creation can involve using biased algorithms as case studies. This approach promotes a deeper understanding of how technology impacts society and underscores the importance of questioning assumptions.

Encouraging Ethical Tech Development

You can also leverage discussions on algorithm bias to highlight the ethical responsibilities of those who develop and deploy the technology. By integrating ethics into STEM education, students can learn to consider the societal impacts of their work and strive to create technology that benefits all users equally. This includes understanding diverse perspectives and needs, ensuring that datasets are representative, and continuously testing and refining algorithms to minimize bias.

Promoting Diversity in STEM

Addressing algorithm bias also presents an opportunity to advocate for greater diversity among those who create technology. You can inspire students from underrepresented groups to pursue careers in STEM, emphasizing that their unique perspectives are crucial for developing fair and effective technology. Encouraging a diverse generation of technologists can help reduce bias in future algorithms and ensure that technology reflects the needs and experiences of a broad spectrum of society.

Leveraging Technology for Personalized Learning

Algorithms, despite the challenges of bias, can support personalized learning effectively if designers prioritize fairness and inclusivity in their creation. You can explore and advocate for educational technologies that adapt to each student's learning style and needs while being transparent about how data is used and ensuring that all students benefit equally.

Engaging With the Tech Community

Finally, you can engage directly with the tech community, participating in discussions about algorithm bias and advocating for change. This could involve partnering with tech companies to provide real-world learning experiences for students, contributing to developing more equitable technologies or conducting research to understand further and mitigate the impacts of bias in educational software.

Algorithm bias is a significant challenge, but it also offers a rich opportunity for learning and growth. By addressing this issue head-on, you can help mitigate the negative impacts of biased technology and empower students to become thoughtful, ethical participants in the digital world. Through critical thinking, inclusivity, and engagement with the broader tech community, educators and students can work toward a future where technology serves the needs of all individuals fairly and equitably.

CHALLENGE 6: OVERRELIANCE ON TECHNOLOGY

In today's digital age, technology has undoubtedly revolutionized education, offering countless opportunities for enhanced learning experiences. However, with the proliferation of technology in classrooms, there comes a significant challenge: overreliance on technology. Awareness of the considerable risks of overreliance on technological tools and platforms is crucial.

Relying too much on technology can hinder the development of essential skills in students, like problem-solving and critical thinking. When students become accustomed to relying on technology for every aspect of their learning, they may struggle to develop these essential cognitive abilities. Instead of actively engaging with course material and grappling with complex concepts, students may passively consume information provided by technology, limiting their ability to think critically and independently.

Relying too much on technology can also make it harder to adapt and be resilient when challenges arise. Students accustomed to technology seamlessly providing answers and solutions may need help when faced with situations where technology is not readily available or cannot provide the necessary support. This can impede their capability to tackle real-world challenges and work effectively with others.

Another concern with overreliance on technology is the potential for students to become disengaged or distracted. While technology can be a powerful tool for learning, it also presents numerous distractions, such as social media, gaming, and web browsing. Excessive time spent by students on digital devices can split their attention, resulting in lower focus and productivity in the classroom.

Opportunity: Cultivating Critical Thinking and Teacher Intervention

Despite these challenges, overreliance on technology allows you to cultivate critical thinking skills and intervene to ensure optimal learning experiences for students.

Incorporating more active learning strategies into the classroom, such as encouraging students to engage in discussions, debates, and hands-on activities, can address the overreliance on technology. This approach fosters critical thinking and problem-solving skills. By shifting the focus from passive information consumption to active engagement with course material, you can empower students to think critically and develop a deeper understanding of key concepts.

Furthermore, you are crucial in reviewing and refining AI-generated content to ensure its educational value. While technology can automate certain aspects of the teaching process, you must provide oversight and guidance to ensure that the content aligns with curriculum objectives and promotes meaningful learning outcomes. You can curate and customize digital resources to meet the diverse needs of your students and supplement traditional instruction with technology-enhanced learning experiences.

Additionally, you can model and encourage responsible technology use among students. Teaching students digital literacy skills and fostering digital citizenship can equip them to navigate the digital terrain responsibly and ethically.

By promoting critical thinking, problem-solving, and digital literacy skills, you can empower students to thrive in an increasingly technology-driven world while minimizing the risks associated with overreliance on technology.

While technology offers tremendous potential to enhance learning experiences, you must be mindful of the risks associated with overreliance on technology. You can leverage technology's potential to foster valuable learning experiences and equip students for success in the digital era by developing critical thinking skills, overseeing AI-generated content, and encouraging responsible technology usage.

CHALLENGE 7: LACK OF HUMAN CONNECTION AND EXPERIENCE

Today's digital era has completely transformed our way of connecting through the widespread adoption of technology. While advancements in AI have undoubtedly brought convenience and efficiency to various aspects of our lives, they also pose significant challenges to human connection and experience. We must recognize and address these challenges effectively to ensure our students thrive in a digital world.

The Rise of AI and Its Impact on Human Connection

Almost every aspect of our daily lives now incorporates AI, from virtual assistants such as Siri and Alexa to recommendation algorithms on social media platforms. While these technologies offer unparalleled convenience and efficiency, they also have the potential to intensify and worsen the public health crisis of loneliness, isolation, and lack of connection.

One of the primary ways AI exacerbates this issue is through its ability to personalize and customize user experiences. While this might appear advantageous initially, it also risks fostering echo chambers. In such environments, individuals only encounter information and viewpoints that mirror their beliefs and values. As a result, people may become increasingly isolated from differing viewpoints, hindering meaningful dialogue and connection.

Furthermore, the rise of AI-powered communication tools like chatbots and virtual assistants may inadvertently diminish opportunities for genuine human interaction. While these tools can provide immediate assistance and support, they lack the empathy, understanding, and emotional connection only human interaction can provide. Over time, prolonged reliance on AI-driven communication may lead to feelings of loneliness and alienation, particularly among vulnerable populations such as older people or individuals with disabilities.

Addressing the Challenge: Opportunities for Better Learning and Growth

While the proliferation of AI presents significant challenges to human connection and experience, you have a unique opportunity to leverage technology to foster genuine connections and meaningful learning experiences.

Emphasize Digital Literacy and Critical Thinking Skills

Incorporate lessons on digital literacy and critical thinking skills into your curriculum to help students navigate the digital landscape responsibly. Teach them to critically evaluate online information, recognize bias and misinformation, and engage in respectful and constructive online discourse. By empowering students with the skills to navigate digital spaces effectively, you can help mitigate the adverse effects of AI on human connection.

Foster Collaborative Learning Environments

Let's generate opportunities for learning together, both online and offline. Encourage group discussions, peer-to-peer collaboration, and project-based learning activities that require students to work together toward a common goal. You can help students develop essential interpersonal skills and cultivate meaningful connections with their peers by fostering community and collaboration.

Integrate Technology Mindfully

Integrate technology into your teaching practices mindfully, ensuring that it enhances rather than replaces human interaction. Use AI-powered tools and platforms to facilitate learning, provide personalized support, and prioritize opportunities for face-to-face interaction and real-time feedback. Incorporating technology and traditional teaching methods can uphold a sense of human connection and cultivate greater student engagement.

Promote Empathy and Emotional Intelligence

Emphasize the importance of empathy and emotional intelligence in online and offline interactions. Motivate students to engage in exercises that actively cultivate skills in listening, understanding different perspectives, and fostering empathy to enhance their ability to connect with others. By nurturing these interpersonal skills, you can help students cultivate meaningful relationships and navigate digital spaces with empathy and compassion.

Create Safe and Inclusive Spaces

Establish safe and welcoming environments for students, ensuring they feel valued, respected, and supported. Cultivate a classroom atmosphere that embraces diversity, fosters open communication, and encourages mutual respect among all students. By creating an environment where all voices are heard and respected, you can help students develop a sense of belonging and connection that transcends the limitations of AI-driven communication.

Opportunity: Leveraging AI for Social Good

While AI challenges human connection and experience, it also presents opportunities for positive social impact. By harnessing the power of AI for social good, you can leverage technology to address pressing social issues, promote equity and inclusion, and foster meaningful connections within your communities.

One example of leveraging AI for social good is using chatbots and virtual assistants to provide mental health support and resources to needy individuals. Organizations like Crisis Text Line and Woebot utilize AI-driven chatbots to offer immediate emotional support and connect individuals with resources and services for mental health and well-being. AI-powered platforms can offer accessible and anonymous support, allowing organizations to communicate with individuals who might not have access to conventional mental health services and support networks.

AI-powered platforms enable organizations to provide accessible and anonymous support, facilitating connections with individuals who may lack access to traditional mental health services and support networks. AI algorithms in platforms such as Google Translate and Microsoft Translator facilitate real-time text and speech translation, empowering people of diverse linguistic backgrounds to communicate fluently and access information in their preferred language. By breaking down language barriers, these tools promote inclusivity and foster connections among individuals from diverse cultural and linguistic backgrounds.

Additionally, AI can personalize learning experiences and assist students with various learning needs. AI algorithms in adaptive learning platforms like Khan Academy and Duolingo analyze student performance to offer personalized recommendations and feedback tailored to individual learning styles and preferences. This customization optimizes learning outcomes and fosters academic success for every student.

It's essential to recognize the potential of AI to drive positive social change and actively engage with technology in ways that promote equity, inclusion, and connection within our communities. By leveraging AI for social good, we can harness the power of technology to address pressing social issues, empower individuals, and build a more connected and inclusive society.

KEY TAKEAWAYS

- Protecting sensitive student information is crucial in today's digital age.
- Establishing robust security measures and ensuring compliance with data protection regulations is crucial.
- Workshops and information sessions that empower students and parents cultivate a sense of responsibility.
- Continuous improvement is essential to staying abreast of evolving threats and challenges.
- Economic disparities and geographic challenges contribute to unequal access to technology.
- Creating partnerships between communities and private entities can supply resources for schools and students facing needs.
- Adopting flexible learning models and technology lending programs ensures equal opportunities for all students.
- Providing digital literacy training for students, teachers, and parents empowers the entire school community.
- Advocating for policy change at all levels prioritizes funding and support for technology access in education.
- Discerning the reliability of information is paramount in the digital age.
- Encouraging students to evaluate sources and promoting information literacy nurtures critical thinking abilities.

- Fostering a questioning mindset and engaging in real-world problem-solving activities encourages skepticism and curiosity.
- You can foster integrity through clear policies, teaching critical research skills, and promoting a culture of accountability.
- Algorithm bias in technology reflects human prejudices and can perpetuate inequalities, especially in education.
- Addressing algorithm bias involves teaching critical thinking, emphasizing ethics in tech development, and advocating for diversity in STEM.
- Overreliance on technology in education can hinder critical skill development and engagement.
- You can mitigate overreliance by promoting active learning, monitoring AI-generated content, and teaching responsible tech use.
- Lack of human connection due to AI can lead to loneliness, but you can promote empathy and inclusivity to counteract this.
- Leveraging AI for social good involves using technology to provide mental health support, break down language barriers, and personalize learning experiences.

CONCLUSION

As we close this enlightening journey, remember that embracing AI in education isn't about the tech alone. It's about you and the vibrant, engaging learning environments you create. This book has armed you with tools and strategies; now imagine the possibilities. But first, let's review what you learned.

EDUCATION IN THE AGE OF AI

In this chapter, we dove into the essentials of AI, aiming to equip you with the knowledge to navigate how AI is revolutionizing education. You learned that AI isn't just a buzzword but a tool reshaping how we teach and learn, making your role as an educator even more pivotal. We explored examples showing AI's impact, from personalized learning paths to automating administrative tasks, freeing you to focus more on what you love—teaching and inspiring students.

You also saw how AI is not here to replace you but to support and enhance your teaching methods, making education more accessible and engaging for every student. By understanding AI's capabilities and limitations, you're better prepared to integrate these technologies into your teaching strategies, making learning more effective and enjoyable.

AI-INTEGRATION METHOD 1—STREAMLINING LESSON PLANNING

In this chapter, you discovered practical strategies for leveraging AI to enhance and simplify lesson planning. You explored a curated list of AI tools and learned how to integrate them into your lesson-planning process seamlessly. This approach improves both efficiency and innovation, raising the level of education for both you and your students.

You found that using AI tools for lesson planning isn't just about saving time and enriching your teaching methods. These tools offered ways to customize learning experiences to meet the unique needs of each student, suggesting activities and resources that cater to diverse learning styles.

By now, you've seen firsthand how AI can transform the mundane tasks of lesson planning into opportunities for creativity and engagement. You've learned to use AI not as a replacement for the human touch in education but as a supplement that enhances your ability to connect with and inspire your students.

The strategies provided here aim to support you in navigating the vast landscape of AI tools, equipping you with the knowledge to select and apply these technologies in ways that make your teaching more impactful. As you experimented with different AI applications, you streamlined your workflow and opened new pathways for your students to explore and learn.

AI-INTEGRATION METHOD 2—ENHANCING EXAM AND ACTIVITIES CREATION

In this chapter, we dove into practical strategies for using AI to revolutionize the way you create student activities, such as exams and homework. We explored a variety of AI tools, guiding you on how to integrate them seamlessly to design assessments that effectively measure student understanding while fostering a dynamic learning environment.

You discovered how to use AI for crafting personalized quizzes that adapt to each student's learning pace, ensuring that assessments challenge yet accommodate all levels of understanding. We spotlight adaptive learning platforms that dynamically adjust question difficulty based on student responses in real time, aligning with their current skill levels.

Moreover, we showed you how to employ AI to generate creative homework assignments that encourage critical thinking and problem-solving. By leveraging natural language processing, you can create open-ended questions that inspire students to think outside the box, making learning more engaging and enjoyable.

We also touched on the importance of feedback, introducing AI systems capable of providing instant, constructive feedback on student submissions. This accelerates the learning process and frees up your time to focus on in-depth, personalized teaching.

AI-INTEGRATION METHOD 3—REVOLUTIONIZING GRADING AND ASSESSMENT

This chapter looked at practical strategies that empower you to harness AI for enhancing grading and assessing your students' performance. Imagine dedicating less time to grading papers and exams and more to crafting an engaging, personalized learning experience for your students. AI tools have made this not just a possibility but a reality for educators around the globe.

We explored a curated list of AI tools specifically chosen to enhance education. These tools can automatically grade multiple-choice and fill-in-the-blank tests. Some are even sophisticated enough to evaluate short responses and essays. The real magic, however, lies in integrating these technologies into your classroom to offer timely, personalized feedback to each student.

Imagine you've just finished a unit. Now, it's time to evaluate your students' understanding. Instead of spending your weekend grading, you use an AI tool that provides immediate results. But it doesn't stop there. Based on the outcomes, the AI suggests tailored follow-up activities for each student to reinforce concepts or tackle misunderstandings.

Moreover, incorporating AI into your teaching practice encourages a shift from traditional assessment methods to a more formative approach. This means you're not just assigning grades; you're engaging in an ongoing dialogue with your students about their learning journey. By offering personalized feedback and suggesting targeted resources, you guide them in recognizing their strengths and areas needing improvement, encouraging a mindset geared toward growth.

AI-INTEGRATION METHOD 4—RESEARCHING NEW TEACHING MATERIALS AND METHODS

In this chapter, you dove into how AI could revolutionize your approach to sourcing and applying new teaching materials and methods. We walked through a selection of AI tools designed to automate the process of finding resources that resonate with the dynamic needs of your students. Imagine having the power to tailor content delivery in real time, ensuring every lesson hits home. You learned to integrate these tools seamlessly into your daily routine, making the hunt for fresh, relevant teaching aids less of a chore and more of an exciting exploration.

You discovered how AI doesn't just simplify discovery; it personalizes it. By feeding the system data on student performance and preferences, you saw firsthand how the technology could serve up content suggestions that were relevant but also timely and engaging. This continuous feedback loop ensures that your teaching methods evolve alongside your students, keeping you one step ahead in meeting their learning needs.

AI-INTEGRATION METHOD 5—PROVIDING ONE-TO-ONE SUPPORT FOR STUDENTS

This chapter introduced you to effective strategies for leveraging AI to deliver customized support to every student, addressing their specific learning needs and strengths. You learned about a range of AI tools, each selected for its potential to tailor the learning experience to the individual student. When integrated effectively into your teaching practice, these tools can transform the educational journey, making it more customized and impactful for every learner.

You began by identifying your students' specific needs and abilities, using AI to analyze patterns in their learning habits and areas where they might need additional support. From there, you explored various AI applications, from adaptive learning platforms that adjust content difficulty in real time to AI tutors that provide instant feedback on assignments, ensuring that each student receives attention exactly where they need it.

The chapter smoothly explored how to weave these AI tools into everyday teaching practices. You learned tips for blending traditional teaching methods with these innovative technologies, creating a hybrid model that leverages the best of both worlds. This approach allowed you to spend more time on interactive, human-centric teaching while AI took care of personalized content delivery and assessment.

By the end of the chapter, you felt equipped with the knowledge to implement these AI tools effectively, ensuring every student benefits from a learning experience that recognizes and nurtures their potential. This journey into AI-enhanced education not only maximized student engagement and learning outcomes but also reinvigorated your passion for teaching, reaffirming the invaluable role of educators in guiding and inspiring the next generation.

AI-INTEGRATION METHOD 6—AUTOMATING ADMINISTRATIVE TASKS

In this chapter, we dove into practical strategies for you, the educators, to harness AI to take the load off your administrative tasks. We explored a variety of AI tools, each selected for its ability to streamline the more mundane parts of your workload. You learned how to integrate these tools seamlessly, transforming your administrative workflow into something more manageable, efficient, and less time-consuming.

We started with easy-to-use AI-powered grading systems, showing you how to cut down grading time significantly. Then, we moved on to virtual assistants explicitly designed for educational environments, capable of handling scheduling, reminders, and communicating with students about deadlines and assignments.

Attendance tracking saw a revolution, too, with AI tools that automate the process, freeing up minutes at the start of each class that add up over time. We didn't stop there; document management systems got smarter, enabling you to organize and retrieve files with simple voice commands or text searches.

TURNING AI CHALLENGES INTO OPPORTUNITIES FOR EDUCATIONAL GROWTH

Imagine you're standing at the forefront of a rapidly changing educational landscape, where challenges from AI and technology loom large. Instead of viewing these challenges as hurdles, let's see them as stepping stones toward creating a more adaptive, inclusive, and tech-savvy educational environment. As educators and administrators, you stand at the forefront of spearheading this transformative journey.

By embracing AI, you can unlock new ways to enhance the educational experience, making it more personalized and engaging for students. This shift requires a mindset that sees every AI challenge as an opportunity to innovate and improve. As discussed earlier, it's about leveraging AI to automate administrative tasks, freeing up precious time for what truly matters: fostering more profound connections with your students.

Imagine harnessing AI to provide instant assignment feedback, enabling a more dynamic learning process, or utilizing adaptive learning technologies that tailor educational content to meet the unique needs of each student. These are not distant realities but achievable milestones on our journey toward a more effective and responsive educational system.

Embrace these changes with an open heart, ready to try new things and eager to learn. Doing so enhances your student's educational experience and empowers you with new tools and strategies that make teaching more rewarding and impactful.

Imagine teachers like you transforming their classrooms with AI, turning hours of grading into moments of personal growth and paperwork into opportunities for creative lesson planning. Educators across the globe are already writing success stories, harnessing AI to carve out more time for what truly matters: their students. They're not just surviving the technological wave but riding it, enhancing their capabilities, enriching learning experiences, and deepening connections with their students.

Dive into the next chapter of educational evolution by adopting AI. Discover, innovate, and modify your instructional approaches to harness the incredible capabilities of this game-changing technology. Free up valuable time by letting technology handle paperwork, grading, and other time-consuming responsibilities, allowing more time for the heart of your profession—teaching. This is your call to action: Dive into the possibilities AI offers and redefine what it means to teach and inspire.

REFERENCES

Artificial intelligence in education. (n.d.). UNESCO. https://www.unesco.org/en/digital-education/artificial-intelligence

Butler, R. (1988). Enhancing and undermining intrinsic motivation: The effects of task-involving and ego-involving evaluation of interest and performance. *British Journal of Educational Psychology, 58*(1), 1-14. https://doi.org/10.1111/j.2044-8279.1988.tb00874.x

Facts and statistics. (n.d.). International Center for Academic Integrity. https://academicintegrity.org/resources/facts-and-statistics

Hardison, H. (2022, April 19). *How teachers spend their time: A breakdown.* Education Week. https://www.edweek.org/teaching-learning/how-teachers-spend-their-time-a-breakdown/2022/04

Henebery, B. (2023, March 28). *Reducing admin tasks boosts teacher morale, study finds.* The Educator Online. https://www.theeducatoronline.com/k12/news/reducing-admin-tasks-boosts-teacher-morale-study-finds/282229

How AI can transform education for students and teachers. (2023, May 1). The World Economic Forum. https://www.weforum.org/agenda/2023/05/ai-accelerate-students-holistic-development-teaching-fulfilling/

McCarroll, D. (2022, July 6). *New EdChoice report reveals how teachers manage time, distractions, and discipline issues in school.* EdChoice. https://www.edchoice.org/media/new-edchoice-report-reveals-how-teachers-manage-time-distractions-and-discipline-issues-in-school/

Why your students are disengaged. (2022, August 3). Harvard Business Publishing. https://hbsp.harvard.edu/inspiring-minds/why-your-students-are-disengaged

MAKE A DIFFERENCE WITH YOUR REVIEW
UNLOCK THE POWER OF UNDERSTANDING

"Intelligence plus character—that is the goal of true education."

DR. MARTIN LUTHER KING JR.

This profound statement underscores the essence of what we strive for in the educational realm. It is in this spirit of generosity and collective uplifting that I reach out to you today.

My collective goal is to make the insights and strategies within "Integrating AI in the Classroom" universally accessible, empowering educators at every level to revolutionize their teaching methodologies. Achieving this ambitious vision, however, requires reaching an audience as broad and diverse as the educational community itself.

This is where your invaluable contribution comes into play. The influence of your review cannot be overstated; it serves as a beacon for countless educators navigating the vast sea of resources in search of reliable and transformative tools.

By sharing your thoughts and experiences about "Integrating AI in the Classroom," you're not just critiquing a book; you're lighting a path for gifted teachers to better serve their students.

If this book has sparked a flame of inspiration within you, I encourage you to share it.

Simply scan the QR code or follow the link to leave your review:

https://www.amazon.com/review/create-review/?
asin=B0D3Q7NKJS

I eagerly look forward to sharing with you more of the insights and strategies that "Integrating AI in the Classroom" has to offer.

With the deepest gratitude, - JH Madron

9 798330 687572